The DO IT Change Method™

A Practical Framework for Navigating Change
with Confidence, Intention, and Momentum

Janine Lequay

Raven + Grace

Raven + Grace Press

Copyright © 2026 by Janine Lequay

Published by Raven + Grace Press

All rights reserved.

No portion of this book may be reproduced aside from short quotes used for review purposes without written permission from the publisher or author, except as permitted by U.S. copyright law.

For information or permission, contact:

Raven and Grace Press

info@ravenandgrace.com

ravenandgrace.com

ISBN ebook: 979-8-9935494-6-0

ISBN paperback: 979-8-9935494-5-3

The information provided in this book is for educational and informational purposes only and is not intended as medical advice, diagnosis, or treatment. Always seek the advice of a qualified healthcare provider with any questions regarding a medical condition. The author and publisher specifically disclaim any liability, loss, or risk, personal or otherwise, which is incurred as a consequence, directly or indirectly, of the use and application of any of the contents of this book.

No AI Training: No part of this publication may be used or reproduced in any manner for the purpose of training artificial intelligence technologies or generating synthetic content without the express written permission of the author. The author reserves all rights to the use of this work for AI training and data mining, and any unauthorized use shall be considered a violation of the author's copyright.

For every person standing at the edge of transformation,
may you always have
the willingness to seek understanding,
the courage to choose,
and the confidence to DO IT™.

Contents

The Allure of Change	VI
My Story	XVI
1. What Is Change, Really?	1
2. The DO IT Change Method™	16
3. DISCOVER	46
4. OWN	68
5. IMPLEMENT	88
6. TRANSFORM	113
7. Overcoming the Hurdles	140
8. You Got This	153
A Letter of Encouragement	166
Resources & THE DO IT™ Ecosystem	169
Acknowledgements	176
Janine Lequay	180

The Allure of Change

Change has been part of your life since the moment you arrived in this world. It wasn't something you needed to prepare for or overcome. It was simply the rhythm of living. You grew, adapted, learned, and shifted without hesitation because, in those early years, change wasn't something to fear or manage; it was embedded in your nature.

You didn't question whether you were ready to evolve, negotiate with yourself about taking the next step, or critique your reactions. You responded instinctively—rolling over for the first time, learning to crawl, standing, then walking—because movement, growth, and adjustment were woven into the way you were designed to operate.

As you got older, however, the simplicity faded. Life became more layered, and the changes you encountered began to carry weight—real weight. Responsibility settled in, expectations multiplied, experiences accumulated, and your identity solidified. And with all of that, your relationship with change grew more complicated. What once felt natural began to feel disruptive, and what once felt exciting sometimes stirred uncertainty. Even when you wanted a shift, even when you knew something needed to evolve, the emotions surrounding that decision felt heavier than they used to. It wasn't because you became less capable or that you lost your ability to adapt. It was because life now had context, and every change touched multiple parts of who you were.

The truth is, we rarely talk honestly about what change demands from us as adults. We talk about transformation as if it's a motivational moment, a single decisive choice, or a sudden revelation. But real change—the kind that affects your identity, relationships, confidence, direction, and the future you're building—often arrives with layers of emotion and complexity that can't be captured in a quick quote or a catchy slogan.

> You can want change and still feel uneasy.

You can be strong and still feel unsteady. You can be hopeful and still worry about the unknown. You can trust yourself and still feel the weight of everything that a transition touches. None of that indicates a lack within you; it simply reflects that you are human and deeply invested in your life.

After more than fifteen years working in organizational change management and navigating the unpredictable transitions of my personal life, I've come to understand that people don't struggle with change because they are incapable. They struggle because no one has ever taught them how to move through it intentionally. In organizations, we develop strategies, communication plans, readiness assessments, and structured processes to support people through transition. We understand that change impacts emotions, behavior, performance, decision-making, and morale. But in our personal lives—where the stakes may feel even higher—we expect ourselves to navigate the same terrain with little more than instinct and pressure.

We expect ourselves to transition seamlessly, to manage our emotions with perfect composure, and to make sound decisions while everything around us is shifting. We expect ourselves to carry change with grace, without hesitation, without fear, and without ever faltering. Yet if a corporation tried to navigate change without structure, guidance, or a road-map, the entire system would destabilize. Individuals are no different.

> The difference is that we've been conditioned to believe that needing support during personal change is a sign of weakness rather than a natural expression of being human.

That belief is not only unfair; it is unrealistic. And it is exactly why this book exists.

You are here not because you need fixing or correcting, but because change deserves a better approach, one that honors your strength and respects your lived experience, and offers a method that matches the speed and complexity of the world you navigate every day.

Change happens more rapidly than ever before. Careers shift overnight, industries reinvent themselves, relationships evolve, families restructure, and technology is pushing us forward faster than we ever anticipated! And in the midst of all this, life hands us the unexpected—the moments we didn't plan, didn't want, and don't feel prepared to navigate such as the loss of a loved one, layoffs, health crises, relationship ruptures, financial shocks, and identity shifts.

Change does not wait for your schedule to open up. It does not pause while you gather yourself. It does not check in to see whether you feel steady. It arrives when it arrives. And that is exactly why having a method—one that helps you understand your response, regain your footing, strengthen your internal resolve, and move forward with intention—is essential.

The DO IT Change Method™ was created in that space. It wasn't born from theory alone. It emerged from the real intersections of life—the moments when logic and emotion collided, when responsibility and uncertainty clashed, when a chapter closed before a new one was fully visible, and when the next step felt both necessary and overwhelming. I crafted this method because I watched countless people navigate change with determination, yet without support. I watched people with extraordinary potential stumble, not because they lacked strength, but because change interrupted their rhythm and they didn't know how to move through the interruption.

What I learned is that change reveals parts of us we never expected to encounter. It challenges our assumptions, stretches our emotional capacity, and pressures us to decide who we will be on the other side of uncertainty. But change also illuminates strengths we forgot we possessed. It surfaces possibilities we never considered, forces us to reexamine what we truly value, and when we have the right structure guiding us, change becomes less of a disruption and more of a turning point.

This book is not a prescription for who you should become, and certainly is not a demand for perfection or a judgment of how you've handled past transitions.

> It is a grounded, thoughtful, strategic guide that honors the way humans naturally respond to change while giving you a sequence to follow, so you don't lose yourself in the process.

You don't need to be rescued. You don't need someone to tell you what your life should look like. What you need, what we all need, is a rhythm that holds steady when life rearranges itself.

That rhythm is DO IT™.

WHY A METHOD MATTERS

Change becomes even more complex when you consider how much of your identity is shaped by the roles you carry. You may be a parent, a partner, a leader, a friend, a business owner, a caregiver, a student, or the dependable one everyone turns to. You may be the person who holds things together at work, the steady presence in your household, or the one who keeps everything moving behind the scenes. With each role comes a set of expectations—expectations you have of yourself and expectations others have of you. Some are chosen. Some are inherited. Some you didn't even realize you were carrying until you felt the friction of trying to grow beyond them.

So, when change enters, it doesn't simply alter a circumstance—it triggers a transition. Change itself is the event; transition is the internal process that follows. And that internal process doesn't stay contained in one corner of your life. It touches everything connected to you. It influences how you show up in your relationships. It impacts your confidence. It tests your patience. It shifts the way you see yourself. That's why even positive change can feel surprisingly emotional. You might welcome the event, but the transition still asks your mind, your emotions, and your identity to rearrange themselves around it. Every shift has a ripple effect. You don't just move from one situation to another—you bring every layer of your life along with you.

Most people never pause long enough to recognize that difference. They confuse the event with the transition and assume they should be able to move through anything with the same ease they had as children. But adulthood introduces context—history, responsibility, consequences, memories, patterns, fears, dreams, and lived experience—and context makes transition more complex than the change itself. You're not simply adjusting to something new; you're reconciling how that new reality fits into the life you've built, the identity you've formed, and the future you still hope to create.

> That is why change feels so complicated—the event is simple, but the transition is personal, emotional, and deeply human.

When we take this a step further, we realize that change often disrupts the emotional habits you've developed over time. For many people, those habits were formed to keep life manageable. You learn to push through, keep going, stay strong, avoid conflict, or carry the weight silently because that's what life requires at certain moments. But when change sweeps in, those habits don't always support the new direction you're stepping into. And when the old ways of coping no longer work, it can feel like you're losing your footing, even if you haven't done anything wrong.

I've watched high-performing professionals freeze the moment their environment shifted. I've seen confident people question their judgment when their world no longer mirrored the predictability they relied on. I've seen individuals who embody strength suddenly feel unsure not because they became weaker, but because the moment required a different version of their strength—one they hadn't yet practiced. And I've walked through seasons where life required parts of me that I didn't know needed attention, until change exposed them.

These moments don't reveal inadequacy. They reveal opportunity. They highlight areas that are ready to be strengthened, understood, or redirected. They show you where your next level is asking to be built. They invite you to step into a deeper awareness of who you are becoming.

> Without a framework, it can be difficult to separate the natural discomfort of growth from the mistaken belief that you are somehow unprepared.

That misconception is one of the most common barriers people face during change. They interpret uncertainty as weakness and mistake hesitation for lack of readiness. They assume emotional responses mean they aren't capable of moving forward. But uncertainty is not a message that you're unqualified; it's a sign that you're entering territory you haven't yet navigated. And hesitation isn't a warning to retreat; it's simply your mind pausing to assess the path ahead. These are normal human responses. They deserve understanding, not criticism.

The world around us moves so quickly that it's easy to internalize the idea that you should be able to adjust with equal speed. But real adjustment takes time and emotional processing. It takes recalibration and moments of pause. And none of that diminishes your strength. In fact, the ability to pause, reflect, and recalibrate is often what enables you to move forward with confidence instead of rushing into decisions that don't align with who you are.

That is why a method matters.

A method creates structure in moments that feel unpredictable and gives you a sequence to follow when your thoughts are scattered. It keeps you anchored when emotions pull you in different directions and reminds you that your response to change has a rhythm—even if life feels chaotic. And most importantly, it shifts your focus from reacting to leading.

The DO IT Change Method™ does exactly that. It gives you a way to understand what is happening internally, take ownership of your direction, move forward with purpose, and step into the evolution that is already unfolding within you. It doesn't require you to become someone different. It simply helps you access what is already there by guiding you through the natural phases of human transformation.

What has always struck me is how often people endure the hardest seasons of their lives without realizing the strength they were using to get through them. They move through change without acknowledging the resilience and bravery they're actively embodying. I've seen people handle transition with extraordinary courage—courage they couldn't recognize because they were too busy managing the moment in front of them. Those experiences clarified something for me: people don't struggle because they lack capacity; they struggle because they're navigating change without direction.

The reality is, you don't need anyone telling you how to live your life, and you don't need me—or anyone else—dictating your steps. But you *do* deserve support. You deserve a framework that honors your lived experience while strengthening your capacity to navigate whatever comes next. You deserve a method that helps you move through change without losing yourself in the process.

The truth is, change isn't going anywhere. As long as you're alive, you will be evolving, adjusting, stretching, and becoming. Some situations will push you to your limits, and others will pour back into you. Some moments will demand courage, and others will invite confidence. This is the rhythm of growth. And with a method that supports you, change stops being something to endure and becomes something to embrace.

This book is your beginning. The DO IT Change Method™ is your road-map. And the journey ahead is one you are more than equipped to take.

My Story

My relationship with change didn't begin in a classroom or a corporate role. It began in my life, long before I ever imagined I'd build a method around it. Looking back, I can see how every move, career shift, reinvention, financial stretch, and identity pivot quietly trained me long before I had the language for it.

For most of my life, I handled change well. I could adjust quickly, rebuild efficiently, and keep moving even when the path was unclear. People leaned on me because I was steady. Resilience became part of my identity—not the dramatic, "push-through-everything" kind, but the lived kind. The "I'll figure it out" kind.

> But resilience has a shadow side. The same strength that helps you rise can also keep you from noticing when you're carrying too much. For me, that moment arrived the day I was laid off.

After it happened, I didn't fire off applications or scramble to replace what I had lost. On the surface, I stayed calm, too calm. What I interpreted as composure was actually emotional suppression. I was so accustomed to being the steady one that I didn't fully register the impact of losing my job.

Instead of stopping long enough to understand what was happening internally, I redirected my energy. I pursued certifications, enrolled in classes, and began laying the groundwork for a coaching business. Forward movement, in itself, isn't a problem. Momentum matters, and action often creates clarity, but I had skipped a critical step. I was moving without fully understanding my current state, without naming the true impact of the change, and without pausing to define the direction I was actually moving toward. It felt like a pause, but it wasn't grounding. It was motion in a safer direction, progress without orientation.

Still, something meaningful was happening beneath the surface. As I immersed myself in studying change at a deeper level, the early structure of what would eventually become The DO IT Change Method™ began to take shape before I realized I would need it for myself.

I could see the mechanics of change clearly—how people move, look, react, bypass, and avoid. I understood the frameworks and could name the patterns. But I wasn't applying any of it to my own internal world. I was functioning, performing, and producing, but not fully feeling. I was building language for change while remaining disconnected from the emotional truth of my own.

That disconnect didn't announce itself right away. It accumulated quietly. The unacknowledged impact, the unnamed grief, the absence of a defined future state all sat beneath the forward motion, unresolved. And eventually, what hadn't been processed demanded to be seen.

That was the moment everything slowed whether I was ready for it or not.

Something finally gave way. The strength I had relied on for years stopped working. The composure I lived from dulled into numbing. And the confidence I projected no longer matched how disoriented I felt inside. For the first time in my life, I couldn't locate the version of myself I had always depended on.

What was unraveling was my identity. Years of emotional suppression had already distanced me from myself. I had been functioning, producing, and holding everything together, but I was no longer rooted in who I actually was. By the time everything broke open, that internal disconnection had been quietly building for years.

When my emotions finally caught up to me, they didn't arrive gently. Years of unprocessed pressure, fear, exhaustion, and expectation surfaced all at once.

During one of the hardest nights, my husband looked at me and asked, "Who are you?"

And in that moment, I realized I genuinely didn't know. The image I had been holding together collapsed because I had spent so long shaping myself around what everyone else needed. Over the years, I had learned to suppress and minimize my emotions, to be the strong one, the flexible one, and the one who made things easier for everyone else.

> What I understand now is this: collapse is not a breakdown of character or strength. It is a moment of reckoning, one that clears what can no longer hold so something real can finally emerge.

In that season, I could no longer rely on resilience, productivity, or instinct. The tools I had always used to move forward weren't enough. I needed something steady, honest, and grounding—something that could help me understand what was actually happening beneath the surface rather than push me past it.

That was when DO IT™ shifted from a framework I understood professionally to a method I had to lean on personally. It became the structure that helped me name my current state, acknowledge the true impact of what I was experiencing, take responsibility for how I was showing up, and move forward with intention instead of survival. It gave me a way to rebuild by staying present with who I was becoming.

DO IT™ supported me when I needed structure more than strength. And through that support, I learned how to support myself.

This method was shaped by my education, but refined by my unraveling. Built by my expertise, but clarified by my humanity. It became the bridge between who I had been and who I was becoming. Now I write from a voice grounded in both knowledge and lived truth. This method held me when nothing else did, and it exists to hold you too.

Chapter 1

What Is Change, Really?

Understanding the Human Side of Transformation

Change is one of the few experiences every human shares, yet it remains one of the most misunderstood. Many people describe themselves as "bad with change," as if their reactions reveal weakness rather than a natural response to a shifting reality. But the more I've worked with individuals and organizations—and the more I've lived through my own seasons of disruption—the clearer it becomes that people don't struggle with *change* itself. They struggle with *what change touches*.

Change, on its own, is neutral. It isn't personal or emotional until it intersects with your life. A layoff, breakup, diagnosis, relocation, promotion, the birth of a child, a financial shift, or a moment of truth in a relationship are all events. They are external moments when something moves from what it was to what it is now.

But the event is never the full picture. What gives change its emotional weight—what makes it feel heavy, hopeful, disruptive, exciting, or destabilizing—is how that event interacts with your identity, responsibilities, patterns, memories, and the emotional landscape you've developed over time. This is where confusion begins: People assume the event is the hard part, when in reality, the event is only the catalyst.

The complexity lies in the transition.

> Change is the event. Transition is the process. Transformation is who you become because of it.

Change signals an external shift; transition is the internal reorganization that follows. Transition touches every part of your life. It influences how you show up in relationships, impacts your confidence, challenges long-standing patterns, disrupts routines, stretches your capacity, and reshapes the way you interpret your world. It is the emotional, mental, and behavioral process of integrating a new reality into the life you already have.

This is why change cannot be reduced to a simple before-and-after moment. You don't move from employed to unemployed without also navigating questions of identity, financial recalibration, disrupted routines, and the emotional processing that comes with uncertainty. You don't relocate to a new city without moving through unfamiliarity, rebuilding community, adjusting expectations, and rediscovering who you are in a new environment. You don't end a relationship without encountering grief, self-reflection, detangling routines, and redefining what partnership means to you.

Even positive changes—opportunities, promotions, expansions—require transition. Excitement and anxiety can coexist. Growth and fear can coexist. A new reality may be welcome, but it still requires adjustment.

This is why change feels layered: The event is straightforward, but the transition it triggers is intricate and deeply human. And this is where most people struggle because they've been conditioned to pay attention to the event and overlook the process. They assume change is complete the moment it happens, when in truth, the event is only the starting point.

> The real work—the emotional grounding, the mental recalibration, the behavioral shifts, the identity evolution—lives within the transition.

Transition is the process. Transformation is the outcome.

The Three Types of Change

Your reactions to change are not signs of inadequacy; they are reflections of how deeply you are connected to your life, your roles, your identity, and the expectations you carry. That is why the same event can feel manageable to one person and overwhelming to another. It isn't just about capability; it's about *context*.

To understand this, you must recognize that change is not a single experience. It arrives in different forms, each carrying its own emotional signature and internal demands. Most people assume change is either expected or unexpected, but there is a third category that deserves its own space, the kind of change that shakes you from the inside out.

These three types of change—Anticipated Change, Unexpected Change, and Life-Altering Change—shape our reactions far more than we realize. They determine how much emotional bandwidth is required, how quickly or slowly we can adjust, and what internal shifts are necessary to move forward in a steady, grounded way.

Anticipated Change

Anticipated change is the kind you plan for or welcome: promotions, moves you initiate, new opportunities, fresh starts, milestones, etc. These types of changes are growth chapters that reflect expansion. They often come with excitement, optimism, and possibility.

Even anticipated change creates internal tension. The very things you *want* can stretch your emotional capacity because they introduce expectations, raise the stakes, and push you to step into unfamiliar roles. You may feel thrilled and anxious at the same time. You may wake up excited and go to bed wondering whether you can sustain what you're stepping into. That mix of emotions, while contradictory, doesn't mean the change is wrong; it means it matters.

Unexpected Change

Unexpected change arrives without warning. Job loss. Financial strain. Relationship shifts. Health news. Opportunities that appear at inconvenient moments. These changes interrupt your rhythm and force you to adjust faster than you would choose.

The emotional response is often confusion, heightened alertness, or a sense of disorientation because your mind is working overtime to assess what the shift means for your future. Your stability was interrupted, and your reaction reflects that significance.

Life-Altering Change

Then there are the moments that don't just disrupt your plans—they reconstruct your path. These are the losses, turning points, emotional ruptures, or crises that rearrange your identity, routines, relationships, and the version of yourself you've relied on for years.

Life-altering change shakes you because it affects multiple layers of your life at once. It touches who you are, how you think, how you function, and how you relate to the world around you. These changes require recovery, not just adjustment. They ask for reinvention, not simple reorganization.

This category of change is why many people misinterpret their reactions. When your entire life system shifts, it is normal to feel overwhelmed, hesitant, emotional, or unsure. Your reaction isn't an indication of weakness; rather, it's a reflection of the magnitude of what was affected.

Understanding these distinctions free you from the belief that your emotional responses are personal flaws. You react the way you do because change interacts with your life at different levels. Some shifts tap your energy, some tap your responsibilities, some tap your identity, and some tap every part of you at once.

> When you view change through these categories, something powerful happens: You stop judging yourself for your reactions, and you start understanding them.

This awareness doesn't remove the discomfort of change, but it changes the way you interpret what you feel. Suddenly, hesitation, emotional waves, and moments of confusion make sense. Your response is an intelligent, human adaptation to a shift in your world.

The truth is, change doesn't destabilize you because you lack strength. Change destabilizes you because you care about the life you've built.

As life deepens, every shift hits differently. Even the small ones feel bigger, and the big ones reshape you in ways you don't always see coming. And when change starts touching the parts of your life that matter most, instinct and unrealistic expectations of yourself aren't enough. You wouldn't rehab an injury without a physical therapy protocol. You wouldn't train for a marathon without a plan. So why would you navigate an identity-level transition without a guide?

The Psychology Behind Change and Why You React the Way You Do

To understand why change feels the way it does, you have to look beneath the surface—beyond the thoughts you can articulate and into the automatic reactions that unfold in your mind and body before you're even consciously aware of them. People often judge themselves harshly during transitions because they assume their emotional or physical responses reveal something about their capability. In reality, those reactions reveal something far more universal: they reveal how the human brain and nervous system are built.

At its core, the brain's primary job is to keep you alive, not to keep you comfortable. Neuroscientists often describe the brain as a prediction engine. It is constantly scanning your environment, looking for patterns it can rely on. Predictability is the brain's favorite state. When life follows a familiar rhythm, your brain can conserve energy because it knows what to expect. It doesn't need to analyze every detail and it can relax into efficiency.

Change disrupts this efficiency.

When something shifts—whether anticipated, unexpected, or life-altering—the brain exits autopilot and moves into heightened awareness. The amygdala, the part of the brain responsible for threat detection, becomes more active. It's important to understand that "threat" does not mean danger in the dramatic sense. To the brain, a threat can be anything unfamiliar. A new job, a change in routine, a conversation you weren't prepared for, a relationship shift, an unexpected email, anything that alters the predictable pattern can trigger the brain to ask, *"What does this mean for me?"*

The brain doesn't wait for your logical mind to answer that question. It reacts first. You think second.

This is why the initial emotional wave during change can feel disproportionate. Your brain is processing something faster than your thoughts can keep up. The prefrontal cortex—the part responsible for planning, reasoning, and decision-making—tries to step in, but it often lags behind the emotional center. You feel before you understand. This is biology, not inadequacy.

The nervous system also plays a direct role. When life shifts unexpectedly or intensely, your body registers the disruption before your mind creates meaning around it. This may show up as a tight chest, racing thoughts, a sudden drop in energy, restlessness, or an inability to focus. These physical responses are known as *somatic markers*—the body signaling that something important has shifted. Many people mistake these cues as signs they're not handling change well; when in reality, their bodies are simply responding to the sudden break in familiarity.

Your past experiences with change influence your reactions as well. Every transition you have lived through—whether smooth, chaotic, or painful—creates internal reference points. These memories shape your expectations and inform how cautious or confident you feel. They determine how quickly you trust new opportunities or brace yourself for possible loss. This is the brain's associative learning at work when it connects current uncertainty to past emotional experiences to help you interpret what may come next.

For me, that learning didn't show up as hesitation or fear. It showed up as movement. I had navigated enough transitions successfully that my instinct was to act quickly and stay composed. When change appeared, my body recognized it as something survivable, even manageable, and I moved forward without pause. What I didn't recognize at the time was that confidence and readiness can still bypass understanding. My history taught me how to adapt, but it didn't always teach me how to stop long enough to process what a change was actually asking of me.

Behavioral science also points to another powerful truth: uncertainty is more stressful to the brain than negative outcomes. In other words, people often handle "bad news" better than "unknown news." Once the brain understands what it's facing, even if it's difficult, it can form a strategy. But when the outcome is unclear—when you're waiting for results, navigating transition, or anticipating change without knowing where it leads—the brain increases vigilance. This heightened state can feel like anxiety, distraction, irritability, or mental fog. Your brain is trying to gather enough information to restore a sense of grounding.

These biological and psychological responses shape the behaviors people often perceive as "not handling change well." Patterns like freezing, overthinking, hesitating, avoiding, overfunctioning, or temporarily shutting down are not signs of personal failure. They are adaptive responses—old strategies that your mind and body learned long before you consciously recognized them. They developed to help you manage past transitions, protect yourself emotionally, or maintain control when life demanded more from you than you had capacity for.

Understanding this adds a layer of compassion to your experience. You begin to see your reactions as information instead of obstacles. A moment of hesitation tells you your mind is gathering data. A surge of emotion tells you the change touches something meaningful. A dip in energy tells you your nervous system is overwhelmed. None of these reactions are proof of inability—they are indicators of internal recalibration.

Personality also plays a role in how you respond. Research shows that some people naturally move toward novelty, while others move toward stability. Individuals high in openness tend to embrace change more readily. Those high in conscientiousness often prefer structure and consistency. Neither pattern is superior. Both serve a purpose. One leans toward exploration, the other toward preservation. The world needs both.

Then consider the roles you carry such as the responsibilities you hold for your family, your team, your relationships, or your community, and the emotional load of change multiplies. People who carry more often feel more. They are not more emotional; they are more aware of the ripple effects. Sociologists and organizational change experts consistently affirm that the more interconnected your responsibilities are, the more deeply change resonates, because its implications extend beyond you.

When you look at change through this scientific and human lens, something important becomes clear:
Your reactions are not character flaws or signs of weakness. They are not evidence that you can't handle change.

> Your reactions are your system—mind, body, and emotion—working exactly as it was designed to work.

And once you understand the purpose behind your reactions, you stop fighting yourself. You stop judging your responses. You stop assuming you should feel differently. Instead, you begin to recognize that your reactions are guiding you.

This shift from self-blame to self-understanding is the foundation for navigating change with intention rather than instinct.

The Myth of "People Don't Like Change" and the Reality of Life's Infrastructure

One of the most persistent myths about human behavior is the belief that people simply do not like change. The phrase is repeated so often that it has become a kind of cultural shorthand. Yet if you look at how humans move through daily life, the idea quickly falls apart. People adapt constantly and almost effortlessly. They adjust to new technology, shift routines when schedules change, absorb unexpected interruptions in their day, evolve their interests, take on new responsibilities, and navigate transitions both large and small without ever identifying the experience as "change."

In reality, humans are remarkably adaptable.
What they actually struggle with is disruption.

This becomes easier to understand when you step back from the individual experience and view life the way an organizational change strategist views a company: as a system rather than a single function. In Organizational Change Management, before any strategic decision is made, we conduct an impact analysis. It assesses which parts of the organization a change will touch, how deeply it will affect processes, people, roles, communication flows, and dependencies, and what downstream consequences might occur. We never treat a change as an isolated event. We evaluate its ripple across the entire enterprise.

A person's life functions in the same way, even if we don't formally label it.

Imagine a life as a city, made up of an intricate, interconnected infrastructure of roads, neighborhoods, power lines, routines, relationships, and responsibilities. Over time, the city develops predictable patterns. Morning and evening flows differ, certain intersections carry more significance, and quieter streets support the larger system without drawing attention. When everything operates as expected, the city runs with efficiency and ease.

But when one road undergoes construction—even a small one—the effects spread. Commutes shift. Side streets overflow. Businesses feel the disruption. Schools adjust. Delivery routes change. The entire city adapts because a single change interacts with multiple elements of the broader system. The disruption is systemic, not emotional.

This is exactly how life works. An anticipated change might resemble planned roadwork. An unexpected change feels like a sudden closure that forces immediate rerouting. A life-altering change is more like the collapse of a major bridge: the kind of structural event that requires redesign, redirection, and rebuilding. In corporate, change management terms, this is a high-impact, high-risk change—one that affects multiple departments, roles, and operations. It is not the change that creates strain; it is the extent of the impact.

This is why everyday adjustments rarely cause distress. They resemble organizational updates that touch one department or one procedure; they do not provoke an enterprise-wide response. But when the change touches identity, stability, relationships, time, resources, or emotional bandwidth, the "impact analysis" reflects a wider footprint. It affects how a person thinks, moves, functions, communicates, and plans. It introduces uncertainty into spaces that were once predictable. And the deeper the impact, the more the individual's internal system must reorganize.

A job change, for example, impacts schedules, finances, family rhythm, self-concept, and energy. It alters the "operating model" of a person's life.

A relationship shift resembles a restructuring; it affects emotional flow, communication patterns, responsibilities, and long-term plans.

A life-altering moment, such as loss, crisis, betrayal, or a deep personal turning point, acts like a high-stakes transformation initiative. It doesn't ask for small adjustments; it asks for reengineering. And just as organizations experience friction when their operating model shifts, humans feel the internal friction of change touching multiple layers of their life.

When you understand change through this lens by using the same principles businesses rely on, the emotional experience finally makes sense. People are not resisting change; they are responding to the breadth of its impact. The fuller a life becomes, the more integrated the systems, relationships, and responsibilities become, and the more profound the ripple when something shifts. This is simply the natural response of a complex system recalibrating.

This is also why a method matters. In organizations, no major change is executed without a plan, strategy, communication approach, support model, and a step-by-step process to minimize disruption and maintain stability. Yet in personal life—where the impact is often greater—we expect ourselves to navigate deep, system-wide changes with instinct alone. The DO IT Change Method™ bridges that gap. It offers the structured, supportive approach that human systems need to transition effectively, without treating individuals as if they should "just adjust" or "be fine."

> Understanding your life as a system, and your experiences of change as system impacts rather than personal deficiencies, sets the foundation for the method you're about to learn.

The DO IT Change Method™ acknowledges the entire infrastructure and gives you a way to move through anticipated, unexpected, and life-altering changes with the same intentionality organizations apply during transformation.

CHAPTER 2

The DO IT Change Method™

A Framework Built for Real Life, Real Emotion, and Real Momentum

The DO IT Change Method™ exists because people deserve what professional organizations already know to provide: a structured approach that respects the psychological, emotional, and behavioral realities of moving through *any* kind of change. It recognizes that change is not a single category; it is a spectrum. Some shifts are intentional and exciting. Some are disruptive and disorienting. Some are transformational and defining. The method honors all of them.

It is structured into four phases—DISCOVER, OWN, IMPLEMENT, and TRANSFORM. Each phase reflects a natural rhythm people move through when life shifts, offering language, direction, and grounding along the way. These phases give you a way to understand where you are and what you need as you move through change with intention.

What makes DO IT™ unique is that it does not separate the internal experience of change from the external demands of life. It does not treat self-awareness and action as two opposing forces. Instead, it brings them into alignment. Regardless of the type of change, the method offers the same steady structure.

This method for change emerged from the space where human complexity meets the unpredictable rhythm of life. And in that space, I began to notice a consistent pattern: People often speak confidently about what they want, yet their words rarely reveal the truth beneath the surface. They say they want success, stability, happiness, love, confidence, or a more fulfilling life, but those desires often lack the depth of definition needed to become real. The language is familiar and socially acceptable, but deeply unexamined. It reflects what society promotes more than what a person has paused long enough to articulate for themselves. As a result, people chase outcomes that were never truly theirs, set goals without grounding in their actual lives, and then blame themselves when the pursuit collapses under its own vagueness.

This disconnect does not only appear in planned or desired change. It also shows up in the moments no one prepares for. The sudden ending. The unexpected phone call. The shift in circumstances that rearranges the landscape of your life before you have time to name what is happening. When unexpected or life-altering change arrives, people are thrust into transitions they did not choose, and the ground they stand on becomes unfamiliar. In moments like these, no amount of ambition or goal-setting helps. Affirmations cannot soften the blow. Vision boards cannot stabilize the internal tremor. What people need is a way to understand what has shifted, how deeply it touches their life, and how to move forward when their internal world is still catching up to the external one.

This is where the organizational change lens remains invaluable. In that field, we never treat a shift, planned or unexpected, as a simple adjustment. We examine the ripple: what it touches, who it impacts, and what support will be required. We recognize that even the best strategies falter when the human experience is ignored. We anchor change in reality. We align the current state with the future state before attempting any intervention. And most importantly, we acknowledge that people need structure and support regardless of whether the change was chosen or thrust upon them.

Yet in our personal lives, we rarely extend ourselves the same degree of compassion, structure, or insight. I didn't. Even with a deep understanding of how change works, I expected myself to move forward without the same grace and scaffolding I routinely built into organizational transformations.

When a change was planned, such as moving out of the country, I skipped the grounding work and chased abstract goals, assuming enthusiasm alone would carry me forward. When a change was unplanned, like when I was laid-off, I expected myself to absorb the shock, make sense of the impact, and recalibrate my identity with no framework at all. I carried the emotional weight privately, blaming myself for not adapting quickly enough, not realizing that adaptation itself requires a process. And when a change was life-altering, like when I lost my mom, two weeks after giving birth to my daughter, the absence of structure became even more destabilizing.

What I experienced wasn't unique; it reflected how people respond to change when support and understanding is missing. People are not simply overwhelmed in these moments; they are disoriented. They are navigating an internal earthquake while still trying to function in the external world.

> **DISCOVER, OWN, IMPLEMENT, and TRANSFORM**

DISCOVER centers you in your reality—not the one you wish you had or the one you feel pressured to have, but the one you are truly standing in. OWN builds from there. It's the moment where response becomes a choice. It invites you to decide how you will engage with that reality—to recognize what you can influence, accept what you can't, and reclaim a grounded sense of agency, even in changes you never would have chosen. IMPLEMENT turns choice into aligned movement, action that matches your reality, honors your emotional truth, and moves at a pace you can sustain. TRANSFORM is where the internal shift becomes visible, and the work you've done begins to shape how you live, lead, and show up in the world.

And because it works at that depth, this method isn't for a quick fix or a surface-level shift. It's for people who want to navigate change in a real, honest way. It gives language to what feels chaotic, direction when emotions take over, grounding when the future feels unfamiliar, and structure when instinct can't carry you forward.

Change requires orientation, choice, movement, and integration. That is why DO IT™ is structured as a sequence rather than a set of ideas. Each phase exists for a reason, informed by real patterns I've witnessed repeatedly—in organizations, clients, and even in my life.

DISCOVER
The Grounding Phase

DISCOVER is the beginning because change cannot be navigated until you understand three essential truths: where you are now (current state), how the change is affecting you or will affect you (impact), and the direction you want to move next (future state). DISCOVER grounds you in the full landscape of your reality so your next steps are based on understanding rather than assumption.

To do that, DISCOVER starts with an honest look at your current state such as your emotions, patterns, energy, expectations, responsibilities, and the realities shaping your life. This is where the performance stops. You no longer tell the story that makes you look put-together or the one you think others want to hear. You name what is true.

Next comes understanding the impact of the change. In anticipated change, impact becomes prospective: what will this choice disturb, stretch, or require from you? What internal and external systems will be affected—your finances, habits, support networks, responsibilities, and emotional bandwidth? You allow yourself to acknowledge the full ripple of the change to create clarity.

In unexpected change, this looks like recognizing what the disruption has already touched: your sense of safety, confidence, relationships, daily routines, identity, and stability.

Finally, DISCOVER leads you into defining your future state. This is not a detailed end goal; it is direction. In planned change, the future state reflects your intentional trajectory—what you are building, why it matters, and how it aligns with your values.

In unplanned or life-altering change, the future state is softer, more compassionate and grounded. Instead of "reinventing your life," it might simply be: "I want to feel stable again." "I want to rebuild slowly." "I want to move toward something that supports me." The future state gives purpose to the next step even when you cannot yet see the entire path.

Together, current state, impact, and future state make DISCOVER a clarifying, grounding phase. It shifts change from something disorienting to something you can dissect, understand, and eventually move through.

OWN
The Choice Phase

From the awareness you build in DISCOVER emerges the second phase: OWN—the moment where understanding turns into choice. Ownership is not about blame, self-criticism, or absorbing responsibility for things outside your control. Ownership is about how you choose to show up in light of the change. It is where mindset matters most. It is where you decide how you will meet the moment, and what posture you will take as you move through it.

This is the phase where you differentiate what you can control from what you cannot. Most people enter change by grasping for control, trying to predict every outcome or manage every detail to avoid discomfort. But control is rigid. It demands that life unfold according to a script. Ownership, however, is adaptive. It accepts that not everything will go according to plan and focuses on what can still be influenced. It is the shift from reacting to responding, from spiraling to stabilizing, from waiting to engaging.

In OWN, you recognize the power of choice. You can interpret the change as a threat or an opportunity. You can lean into proactive action or retreat into reactive fear. You can let circumstances dictate your energy, or you can decide how you want to meet them. This is where you say, *"This is my life. I get to choose my posture."*

Ownership empowers you to reclaim your position in the center of the change rather than being swept to the edges of it.

When you embrace ownership, you stop letting circumstances write the entire story. You begin writing your part again. Even the smallest choices—setting a boundary, communicating clearly, pausing before reacting, asking for support, or giving yourself grace—shape the trajectory of what comes next.

DISCOVER and OWN together form the internal foundation of DO IT™. They create truth, agency, stability, and alignment. Without them, action becomes rushed, reactive, or misdirected. With them, movement becomes intentional and grounded.

IMPLEMENT
The Movement Phase

Implementation is where movement begins. Many people believe they must wait until everything feels aligned before taking action, but clarity is not the prerequisite for action; it is the result of it. IMPLEMENT honors the truth that you understand life best by living it, not by thinking your way through it.

This phase is not defined by dramatic leaps. Implementation thrives through small, grounded actions that illuminate the next step. You send the email. You explore the option. You ask the question. You organize the task. You make the call. Each action generates information—what resonates, what drains you, what aligns with your future direction, what needs refining. You begin to see the path one step at a time.

Implementation is iterative. When something unexpected arises—new information, an emotional trigger, or a logistical disruption—the method invites you to return to DISCOVER and OWN before moving forward again. IMPLEMENT is the balancing point between doing and learning. You act, you observe, you adjust. You participate in your change rather than waiting passively for certainty.

Over time, these steps accumulate. Momentum forms as you begin to trust your ability to move through uncertainty one honest action at a time.

TRANSFORM
The Integration Phase

Transformation is not the dramatic before-and-after narrative people imagine. It is the gradual alignment that happens after you have moved through the earlier phases with honesty and intention. TRANSFORM is the phase where the change becomes integrated, where what once felt uncomfortable or foreign becomes familiar and natural.

You often notice transformation in subtle ways. You respond differently to situations that once triggered you. You make decisions with more confidence. You set boundaries with ease. You feel a quiet steadiness where there was once overwhelm. You recognize that you've grown because you navigated the process with presence and intention.

TRANSFORM is not about becoming someone entirely new. It is about becoming a version of yourself shaped by truth, choice, action, and growth. It is about seeing yourself clearly and moving through the world with a deeper sense of self-trust.

TRANSFORM completes one cycle of change and prepares you for the next. Life will continue to shift—sometimes gently, sometimes abruptly. But now you have a rhythm for navigating it. When the next transition arrives, you will return to DISCOVER with more honesty, to OWN with more confidence, to IMPLEMENT with more courage, and to TRANSFORM with more ease.

Five Real-World Examples of DO IT™ in Action

To bring this rhythm to life, here are examples of how DO IT™ meets you in different moments of disruption.

EXAMPLE 1 — ANTICIPATED CHANGE (Financial Planning)

"I need to get my finances under control."

DISCOVER

You begin by acknowledging your current state: your spending feels scattered, bills sneak up on you, and you're tired of feeling anxious every time you check your bank account. You admit you've been avoiding the reality because your finances feel overwhelming. Then you look at the impact.

Your financial stress affects your mood, sleep, relationships, confidence, and the way you make decisions. You recognize the anticipatory impact as well—the longer you ignore the problem, the heavier it gets.

Next, you define your future state clearly and realistically:
"I want to feel in control of my money."
"I want to build stability."
"I want to stop living paycheck to paycheck."

DISCOVER takes something vague and turns it into something concrete.

OWN

Ownership is where you choose how you're going to show up in this change. You acknowledge what you *can* control—your spending habits, your budgeting, your planning—and what you *can't* control: unexpected expenses, the economy, or the financial habits of others around you.

You can keep avoiding your finances, overspending when you're stressed, letting bills surprise you, and continuing the cycle of anxiety every month, or you can decide to face this moment with intention. You choose to see this as an opportunity to create freedom and stability, saying, "*This is my money and my future. I get to take ownership of it.*"

IMPLEMENT

You start with small steps:

You review your bank statements.

You total your monthly expenses.

You create a simple budget without overcomplicating it.

You choose one area to reduce spending.

You set up autopay for two recurring bills.

Each small action gives you more clarity about where your money goes and what adjustments matter most.

You continue:

You build a modest savings plan.

You automate transfers.

You pay down one debt at a time.

You track progress weekly, not obsessively, but intentionally.

Implementation becomes a rhythm of active participation.

TRANSFORM

Transformation appears when financial stress stops dominating your thoughts.
It's the moment you pay a bill without panic.
It's the confidence that grows when you see your savings increasing, even gradually.
It's the peace you feel from knowing where your money is going.
It's the pride you feel when you notice you're making intentional financial choices instead of emotional or impulsive ones.

You begin to trust yourself with money in a way you didn't before. Your finances change, and more importantly—you change.

EXAMPLE 2 — ANTICIPATED CHANGE (Relocation)

"I'm thinking about moving to a new city."

DISCOVER

Start by acknowledging your current state: life feels too small, too familiar, or too predictable. You sense that you've outgrown your environment. Your days feel repetitive, and although nothing is "wrong," something inside you longs for more creative space, opportunity, or alignment with who you're becoming.

Then you analyze the impact of exploring a move. You imagine the practical disruptions—leaving your support circle, adjusting to a new cost of living, the logistics of a move, the emotional discomfort of starting over. You also consider the anticipated impact of staying: growing resentment, feeling stagnant, missing out on a chapter that feels meant for you.

As part of DISCOVER, you begin researching possible cities. You look at neighborhoods, job markets, community life, and lifestyle fit to understand what each option requires. One city stands out. The more you learn, the more something inside you settles.

You define your future state:

"I want to live somewhere that stretches me."

"I want to feel energized by my surroundings."

"I want to grow."

DISCOVER creates clarity. And because of that clarity, the decision to move becomes grounded, not impulsive.

OWN

Ownership is how you choose to show up now that the reality of this decision is clear. You acknowledge what you can control—your preparation, your financial planning, your communication, your research—and what you cannot control: the job market, the pace of relocation, or how smoothly the transition unfolds.

You can let the move overwhelm you, second-guess your decision, overthink every unknown, and delay taking action because the process feels big, or you can decide to approach this change with intention.

You choose to treat this move as an opportunity you created for yourself, saying, "*I'm approaching this change with curiosity and grounded intention.*"

IMPLEMENT

You begin with small, grounded steps. You update your resume. You connect with two people who live in that city. You begin applying strategically. You map out a savings plan. You schedule a visit to walk the streets, feel the environment, and see whether the imagined future aligns with the real one.

Every step gives you information.
Each action sharpens the path.
You realize that clarity was built through movement.

Soon, you land an interview that feels right. Then a job offer. Or you commit to relocating first and job searching from the ground. Either way, movement carries you forward.

TRANSFORM

Transformation begins once you arrive. The city feels unfamiliar at first, but slowly you begin weaving yourself into it. You find a grocery store that feels comfortable. You build a routine. You meet people who stretch you. You walk without GPS. You begin seeing the city not as "new," but as "mine."

Internally, something shifts too. You feel more grounded in your capacity. More connected to who you're becoming. More confident in your ability to create a life, not just live one.

You didn't just move cities. You expanded your identity.

EXAMPLE 3 — UNEXPECTED CHANGE (Job Loss)

"I was laid off today."

DISCOVER

You begin by naming your current state: shock, fear, and the sudden loss of a structure you relied on. You feel the emotional sting of uncertainty, embarrassment, anger, or a sense of failure. Then you examine the impact. The layoff affects your schedule, finances, identity, stability, confidence, and your relationships. You also look ahead at the anticipated impact of job searching, adjusting your budget, and explaining the situation to your family.

You define a grounded future state:
"I want stability."
"I want meaningful work."
"I want to feel grounded again."

DISCOVER shifts the moment from uncertainty to empowerment.

OWN

Ownership becomes the moment you choose how you will show up in the aftermath.

You cannot control the company's decision, but you can control how you respond to it. You identify what is within your influence such as your résumé, network, communication, and emotional regulation—and what is not: the job market, the hiring timeline, or how others interpret layoffs.

You can spiral into panic, feel powerless in the uncertainty, delay your job search because you feel overwhelmed, and replay the decision in your mind until you're emotionally frozen, or you can decide to approach this moment intentionally.

You choose to see the layoff as a turning point; you still have influence by saying, "*This happened, and I still have a say in what comes next.*"

IMPLEMENT

The movement begins with one small action:
You tell one trusted person.
You review your finances.
You update your LinkedIn profile.

You reach out to colleagues.

You send your first application.

Each step generates data—what roles excite you, which industries you're drawn to, where you feel underqualified or overqualified. Implementation becomes a series of grounded movements that reveal the path.

Some days feel productive. Others feel heavy. Both count as progress.

TRANSFORM

Transformation shows up quietly. You begin speaking about the layoff without shame. You rediscover strengths you forgot you had. You interview with more confidence because you now understand your value in a deeper way. You land a new job or a new direction that aligns with who you are today, not who you were when you accepted the previous role.

The loss that felt destabilizing becomes a turning point you navigated with intention.

You didn't just recover—you rebuilt with purpose.

EXAMPLE 4 — LIFE-ALTERING CHANGE (Grief)

"My significant other passed away unexpectedly."

DISCOVER

Your current state is raw: grief, shock, disbelief, and the sudden collapse of the future you imagined. Your emotional world is shaken, and your physical environment feels unfamiliar without them. You examine the impact—not just emotional, but logistical, relational, structural. This loss touches everything: routines, identity, finances, family dynamics, holidays, and the way you move through each day.

You define a future state that honors your humanity:
"I want to survive this."
"I want to find stability again."
"I want to rebuild slowly with support."

DISCOVER gives shape to what feels uncontainable.

OWN

Ownership here is tender. You are not taking responsibility for the loss; you are taking responsibility for your healing.

You can pressure yourself to "stay strong," avoid your grief out of fear it will consume you, isolate because you don't want to burden anyone, and judge yourself for not healing quickly enough, or you can decide to meet yourself with compassion.

You choose to honor your emotions at your own pace, saying, *"I will move through this with tenderness, not judgment."*

IMPLEMENT

Your steps are small, but they matter.
You get out of bed.
You take a shower.
You eat something nourishing.
You call a friend.
You schedule therapy.
You manage one household task.
You cry when you need to.
You rest when you must.

As time passes, implementation expands. You reengage with the world at your pace. You reconnect with people who feel safe. You begin forming new routines that support the present.

Action doesn't heal the grief, but it helps you carry it.

TRANSFORM

Transformation in grief is not about "moving on."
It is about continuing forward.

It appears when your heart softens for a moment.
When a memory makes you smile before it makes you cry.
When you begin imagining a future again, not in betrayal of what was lost but as a continuation of your strength.

Transformation is integration: the love, the loss, the resilience, and the self you are becoming now.

You didn't just endure the change. You rebuilt a life within it.

EXAMPLE 5 — LIFE-ALTERING CHANGE (Medical Diagnosis)

"*I was just diagnosed with a chronic condition.*"

DISCOVER

Begin by acknowledging your current state of fear, confusion, disbelief, and the sense that your life has just shifted into "before" and "after." You name the emotional impact, the grief for the version of your body you thought you had, anxiety about the future, anger that this is happening, and the exhaustion of not knowing what comes next.

Then you examine the full ripple of the diagnosis: it affects your routines, your energy, your independence, your relationships, your long-term plans, your confidence, and your day-to-day functioning. You also consider the anticipated impact such as treatment schedules, lifestyle changes, medical costs, possible limitations, and the learning curve of managing a condition you never wanted.

You define a compassionate future state:
"I want to understand what my body needs."
"I want to manage this with support, not fear."
"I want to build a life that honors my health."

DISCOVER does not remove the weight of the diagnosis, but it gives the moment structure instead of despair.

OWN

Ownership in a medical diagnosis is where many people get stuck because it is deeply misunderstood. OWN does not ask you to be positive about something painful. OWN does not ask you to "look on the bright side" or pretend your condition is a gift. And it does not imply you caused this or could have prevented it.

You are not responsible for having the condition. You *are* responsible for how you support yourself within it.

You can let the diagnosis define every part of your identity, ignore your needs out of frustration, search the internet until you're terrified, push your body beyond its limits, and hide your struggle because you fear being seen as weak, or you can decide to support yourself within it.

You choose to partner with your reality in a way that protects your well-being by saying, "*I didn't choose this diagnosis, but I can choose how I care for myself within it.*"

You identify what you can influence—your care plan, habits, lifestyle adjustments, communication, willingness to ask questions—and what you cannot: flare-ups, timelines, unpredictability, or the emotional waves that come without warning.

Ownership here sounds like:
"I will advocate for my health."
"I will allow myself to need help."
"I will learn what supports my body."
"I will not let this condition erase my identity."
"I will meet myself with compassion instead of pressure."

OWN is refusing to let the condition control every part of your life.

DEBUNKING TOXIC POSITIVITY AND MOTIVATIONAL FIXES

A diagnosis doesn't need your positivity, it needs your honesty. Toxic positivity tells people to "stay strong," "be grateful," or "just think positive."
But real change begins with acknowledging what is hard, unfair, heavy, or exhausting.

Motivational slogans also fall short here. Chronic illness cannot be outworked, out-hustled, or out-motivated. This is not about willpower. It's about partnership with your reality, not resistance to it.

DO IT™ meets you exactly where you are and honors the truth of your experience while guiding you toward sustainable, compassionate ways of living within it.

IMPLEMENT

Your steps are small, but meaningful:
You schedule follow-up appointments.
You ask your doctor the questions you avoided before.
You gather your medical records.
You adjust one daily habit to support your body.

You speak with someone you trust.
You begin setting boundaries around your energy.
   Over time, implementation expands:
You build a care team.
You learn your triggers and patterns.
You adopt routines that work with your condition.
Your actions become acts of self-respect, not self-punishment.

   Implementation doesn't heal the diagnosis, but it helps you build stability inside it.

TRANSFORM

Transformation in chronic illness is not about "moving on." It's about moving forward.
   Transformation appears when:
You stop feeling defined solely by the diagnosis.
You trust your body again, even in its unpredictability.
You imagine a future without guilt or fear.
You build routines that support—not strain—you.
You recognize your resilience in adapting with grace.

   Transformation is integration: the diagnosis, the grief, the strength, and the self you are becoming now.

   You didn't choose the diagnosis. But you learned how to live—and still live fully—within it.

Retroactive Use — Understanding Your Past Patterns and Lessons Learned

One of the most powerful elements of the DO IT Change Method™ is its versatility, designed to mirror how life actually unfolds. Traditional models assume you are either moving toward something you've planned or reacting to something unfolding in real time. But human change is rarely that orderly. Life does not pause to give you a clean beginning, midpoint, and end.

Some changes sit far behind you, like moments that happened months or years ago yet still echo through your choices today. These are the experiences you thought you left behind, but their lessons, wounds, strength, and unanswered questions continue to shape how you trust, how you plan, how you connect, and how you interpret the world. Without realizing it, these past chapters often influence how you respond to the ones unfolding now.

Using the DO IT Change Method™ retroactively helps you understand these patterns. When you apply the framework to a previous season of change, you begin to see yourself with a clarity you didn't have at the time. You learn who you were, how you responded, and what outcomes those responses created. This retrospective lens turns past experiences into insight rather than lingering confusion.

In retroactive reflection, DISCOVER invites you to revisit the landscape of your life *then*: what you felt, what you feared, what your circumstances demanded, and how the change impacted your emotional, mental, and practical world. You look back not to judge your past self, but to locate it and understand the reality you were navigating and the pressures you were carrying. You acknowledge what the change touched and how far its effects reached.

OWN, retroactively, becomes an honest acknowledgement of how you showed up in that chapter. You recognize the mindset you carried—whether reactive, hopeful, avoidant, courageous, overwhelmed, or determined. You uncover how you interpreted the change, the beliefs that shaped your decisions, and the ways you used (or didn't use) your agency at the time. This is where patterns begin to reveal themselves: the tendencies you lean toward under pressure, the stories you tell yourself, the emotional habits that guide your responses.

In retroactive use, IMPLEMENT becomes a clear look at what you actually did in response to that change.

What actions did you take?

Which steps helped you move forward?

Which ones kept you stuck?

What decisions created momentum, and which ones created resistance?

> Seeing your past actions laid out through a structured lens helps you understand how you navigate uncertainty, which strategies support you, and which ones need rethinking.

Finally, TRANSFORM reveals itself as the outcome of that chapter, the person you became because of the steps you took. When you reflect on who you were then and who you became afterward, you begin to see your evolution. You notice the resilience you didn't recognize at the time. You see the growth that emerged from your choices. You understand the beliefs, strengths, boundaries, and perspectives that were shaped by that season of your life.

This retroactive lens is powerful because it turns your past into data about your resilience, tendencies, blind spots, and your strengths. You identify what went well, what didn't serve you, and what you would do differently next time. This becomes your personal archive of lessons learned, a guidebook for future transitions.

Retroactive use reinforces one truth:
You have navigated change before.
You adapted, you acted, and you transformed—even when you didn't realize it.

And now, with the DO IT™ Method™, you can take those lessons forward with intentionality and confidence.

EXAMPLE 6 — RETROACTIVE USE

"Looking back, my divorce three years ago changed everything."

DISCOVER (Retroactive)

When you look back at that period of your life, you begin by locating your current state at the time. You remember feeling overwhelmed—part grief, part relief, part fear, and part exhaustion. You recall how unstable your world felt: the shifting routines, emotional waves, logistical decisions, and the pressure of trying to appear composed while everything inside you was recalibrating.

You examine the impact as it truly was back then. The divorce touched more than the relationship itself; it affected your finances, your living situation, your identity as a partner, your confidence, your social circle, even the way you interpreted safety and love. Some impacts were immediate; others revealed themselves over time.

You also remember the future state you hoped for in that moment—maybe it was simply peace, stability, or the ability to get through a week without feeling emotionally depleted. It wasn't a grand vision; it was a desire to feel grounded again.

OWN (Retroactive)

As you reflect, you begin to see how you showed up in that season of your life.

You recall the mindset you carried—some days determined, some days defeated, often oscillating between both. You recognize the moments you leaned into strength, the moments you shut down, and the moments you trusted yourself.

You see the patterns:

You avoided difficult conversations because you were drained.

You carried guilt that wasn't yours to hold.

You over functioned in some areas to compensate for the emotional chaos.

You sought support only when you were completely depleted.

Ownership retroactively helps you name these patterns without judgment. You see your humanity, your effort, your intentions. You acknowledge what was within your influence then, such as your communication, your boundaries, your self-care—and what wasn't: your partner's choices, their emotions, the timing of the ending.

IMPLEMENT (Retroactive)

Now you look back at the steps you actually took during that period:
You filed paperwork.
You found a new place to live.
You restructured your finances.
You leaned on a few trusted friends.
You began therapy.
You created routines to steady yourself.
You gave yourself permission to rest when you needed it.
You made decisions.

You see that implementation wasn't glamorous. It wasn't linear. It was a sequence of small, necessary actions that moved you through a season you didn't feel fully prepared for. But you did move, one honest step at a time.

Each of those steps led somewhere. They shaped your relationship with independence, with emotional resilience, and with your capability.

TRANSFORM (Retroactive)

Finally, you see who you became because of that chapter, a truth you couldn't have named while you were living it.

You became steadier.

You learned your strength doesn't require perfection.

You developed clearer boundaries.

You learned how to trust yourself more deeply.

You rediscovered parts of yourself that had gone quiet in the relationship.

You built a life that reflects your values, not just your circumstances.

You realize the transformation didn't happen all at once. It happened slowly, through decisions you barely remember making and actions you took even when you were tired or afraid.

Looking back through the DO IT™ lens reveals the arc you couldn't see in the moment:

how you navigated the shock,

how you showed up with the capacity you had,

what you did to move forward,

and the person you grew into because of it.

Retroactive DO IT™ becomes your evidence that you navigated a major transition before and that you grew because of it.

It shows you your patterns.

It highlights your strengths.

It captures your lessons learned.

Chapter 3

DISCOVER

The Pause Marks the Beginning

Change does not truly begin with the moment something shifts in your life. It begins with the moment you pause long enough to understand where you actually are. This is the purpose of DISCOVER. It is the phase most people overlook mostly because the world conditions us to move quickly. We are taught to fix, to decide, to take action, to "bounce back," and to stay in motion as proof that we are doing well. Movement becomes a measure of progress, even when that movement is misaligned.

> But action without orientation is just movement. It is following momentum instead of intention.

When you skip the grounding step of DISCOVER, you move through change based on assumptions about how you feel, what you need, what the situation requires, and not what you're actually capable of right now. You move forward without ever checking whether your actions match your reality.

This is the same mistake organizations make when they rush into a large-scale transformation without conducting a current-state analysis. Leadership becomes energized about a new strategy, tool, or structure, and in that excitement, they want the change implemented quickly. But without understanding how people currently work, what systems they rely on, and what challenges exist beneath the surface, the initiative becomes misaligned from the start. The problem becomes that the company never paused long enough to understand the starting point. And when the starting point is misunderstood, everything built on top of it struggles.

The same principle applies on a personal level. Skipping DISCOVER is like noticing your car feels "off" and assuming you know the cause. You guess the alignment is off, so you pay to fix it. The noise stays. You replace the brakes. Still there. You worry it's the suspension and spend even more money trying to solve it.

Then, after all the guessing and unnecessary repairs, you finally get a diagnostic and learn it was a simple wheel bearing the whole time. The issue wasn't your ability to fix the car; it was that you were fixing the wrong thing.

People do this with their lives. They try to "fix" the discomfort of change with any action without discovering what the real issue is. They change jobs when they actually need boundaries. They end relationships when they actually need communication. They push themselves to "stay strong" when what they actually need is rest.

They treat symptoms instead of causes because they never took the time to understand *where they were beginning*.

Another perfect example of this is how people treat medical symptoms. Instead of going to the doctor, they start self-diagnosing. A headache becomes dehydration, so they drink more water. When that doesn't work, they assume it's stress, so they take supplements. Then they try new pillows, new vitamins, new routines—anything to relieve the discomfort—without ever checking the root cause. Only after time, money, and frustration do they finally get medical insight that reveals the real issue.

> This is why DISCOVER matters.
> It ensures you begin the change journey from a place of truth—not urgency, not avoidance, and not assumption.

When you understand your starting point, you gain stability. When you understand the impact of the change, you gain perspective. When you define your direction, you gain orientation. Without this sequence, everything that follows becomes harder because you are doing it without a map.

Just as companies who skip their current-state analysis run into breakdowns later, individuals who skip DISCOVER often find themselves overwhelmed or misaligned. Their struggle is almost always because they never paused long enough to understand where they were starting.

DISCOVER doesn't promise that you'll avoid every detour. Sometimes you will still take the wrong turn or act before you fully understand what you're reacting to. But DISCOVER helps you uncover the root cause and begins to clear the fog. It gives you a clearer way to orient yourself, even when certainty isn't available.

The Current State: Naming What Is True Right Now

Most people believe they know their current state because they can name a single emotion or make a broad statement about their situation. *"I'm unhappy," "I'm overwhelmed," "I'm ready for a change," "I'm tired," "I feel stuck."* These phrases sound like clarity, but they are only headlines. They tell you something is happening, but not what is driving it, where it's rooted, or how far it reaches.

Your current state is more than a feeling; it is a landscape. It is the full picture of what is happening internally and externally—not just what you're aware of in the moment, but what influences you beneath the surface.

In effective organizational change, a current-state assessment never stops at the top. It doesn't rely on leadership's interpretation alone. It moves through departments, teams, processes, workflows, and culture. It looks at how people function, what supports them, what slows them down, and what realities shape their performance. A company that claims, "Morale is low," hasn't named its current state. That's a summary. A real assessment looks at *why* morale is low, where it shows up, how it affects engagement, and what systems or pressures contribute to it.

The same is true for your life. "I'm unhappy" is not a current state. It is an alert, a signal, a headline.

Your real current state exists underneath that sentence.

DISCOVER invites you to go deeper by mapping out the landscape of your reality with honesty, not judgment. It helps you articulate what is actually happening in your world so you can understand the conditions you're moving through.

The Five Layers of DISCOVER

To understand your current state, you explore five layers:

1. *Your Emotional Landscape*

Your feelings are part of your current state, but they are not the whole picture. Emotions give you signals such as fear, excitement, resentment, confusion, hope, anger, numbness, eagerness, and DISCOVER asks you to understand them. **Ask yourself:**

What am I truly feeling right now? Not the polished answer, my honest one.

Are my emotions coming from the change itself or from something I'm afraid the change will reveal?

Which emotions are loudest? Which ones am I ignoring?

What am I carrying that I haven't yet named?

This level gives you a sense of the emotional climate you're operating in.

2. Your Mental Landscape

Your thoughts shape your interpretation of the change. This includes your beliefs, stories, expectations, and the assumptions you've been operating from. **Ask yourself:**

What do I believe about my ability to navigate this change?
What story am I telling myself about what this means?
Where am I assuming danger when there may be none?
Where am I assuming ease where there may be challenges?
What fears or limiting beliefs amplify the situation?
Your mental landscape influences how you feel and behave.

3. Your Circumstances and Responsibilities

Your current state is grounded in your reality—your schedule, financial commitments, relationships, roles, limitations, and your resources. Circumstances force you to look at your life with honesty. **Ask yourself:**

What is happening in my life right now that affects my ability to move through this change?
What responsibilities am I carrying?
What is supporting me? What is draining me?
What practical constraints or obligations do I need to acknowledge?

This layer grounds your understanding in tangible truth, not idealistic hope.

4. *Your Environment and Systems*

The systems and environments in your life influence how any change will land. **Ask yourself:**

What systems in my life help me function well? Which ones break down under pressure?
Who around me influences how I navigate this change?
What habits shape my daily experience?
Does my environment support my growth or inhibit it?

This layer reveals the conditions supporting you or complicating your path.

5. *Your Patterns and Triggers*

Every person has patterns, the ways they react to pressure, uncertainty, or opportunity. Your current state includes those tendencies. **Ask yourself:**

When I'm overwhelmed, what do I usually do? Freeze? Overfunction? Withdraw? Rush?
How have I handled similar changes in the past?
What patterns tend to repeat themselves in moments like this?
What typically triggers strong reactions for me?

Remember: Patterns are data. They help you anticipate your needs as you move forward.

Putting It All Together to DISCOVER

When you combine these five layers, you no longer have a vague statement like, "I'm unhappy." You have a multidimensional, truthful view of where you are—emotionally, mentally, practically, relationally, and behaviorally. This becomes your actual current state.

And with this clarity, everything else becomes easier to navigate. Because you are no longer reacting from instinct or fear; you are responding from understanding.

DISCOVER is not about dissecting your life; it is about orienting it. It helps you see what you're carrying so you can move forward with intention instead of assumption.

This depth of awareness prepares you for the next step: **Impact**, where you examine not just where you are but how the change is reaching into your world.

What a Real Current State Looks Like

To understand how these layers work together, imagine someone saying, "I'm unhappy in my job." At first glance, that seems like a current state. But it's really only a headline. When they move through the layers of DISCOVER, the fuller picture begins to reveal itself.

Emotionally, they may realize they feel anxious every Sunday night, disconnected throughout the workday, and disappointed in themselves for "staying too long." They feel unhappy and carry fear, frustration, guilt, resentment, and exhaustion. These emotions shape how they show up, even if they hadn't named them before.

Mentally, an entirely different set of truths emerges. Their thoughts are filled with worries about making a change. They believe leaving is risky. They assume they won't find something better. They fear disappointing others or making the wrong move. They repeat stories like, "I should be grateful," or, "It's too late for me to start over." These narratives influence their decisions just as much as the job itself.

Circumstances add another layer of reality. Perhaps they're juggling childcare, recovering from a financial setback, or supporting aging parents. Maybe their commute drains hours from their day, or their workload spills into every evening. These practical demands reveal the weight they're carrying as they consider it.

Their environment expands the picture even further. Maybe they work in a culture that normalizes burnout or in a department where recognition is scarce. Perhaps they sit in a cluttered workspace, stare at an overwhelming calendar, or operate in a home environment where support is inconsistent or unavailable. Environments—both at work and at home—shape how safe or sustainable change actually feels.

And then there are the patterns. They might notice they tend to stay in roles longer than they should because uncertainty feels threatening. Maybe they avoid conflict, overextend themselves, or push through discomfort rather than naming it. These patterns act as protective strategies that once kept them safe. But now, those same strategies shape how they navigate this moment.

When these layers come together, the simple headline—"I'm unhappy in my job"—evolves into something far more accurate:

"I'm emotionally drained because I feel undervalued, mentally weighed down by fears of change, carrying responsibilities that limit my bandwidth, navigating environments that don't support my well-being, and repeating a familiar pattern of staying too long because uncertainty feels threatening."

Now *that* is a current state.

> And it's from this level of truth that aligned decisions can be made. From here, they can see what actually needs to shift, what support they require, and what steps make sense for their life. They stop trying to solve the wrong problem and begin addressing what's really happening.

That is the power of DISCOVER: It brings the full truth into view so your next step is grounded instead of guessed.

Impact: Understanding the Ripple, Not Just the Moment

Once you understand your current state, the next layer of DISCOVER is identifying the **impact** of the change. Impact is the ripple effect. For example, how the change reaches into different areas of your life, what it touches, what it shifts, what it disrupts, and what it demands. People often underestimate the importance of this step because they assume the impact is obvious. But the effects of change are almost always broader and deeper than the event itself.

Impact is not how you feel about the change. It is how the change interacts with the structure of your life.

In organizational change, this is known as an **impact analysis**. When companies introduce a new system, process, or structure, a surface-level understanding—*"This will make things better"* or *"This will streamline operations"*—is never enough. Change managers study how the shift affects each department, role, workflow, skill set, timeline, responsibility, and stakeholder. They ask:

Who will be impacted?
How will their work change?
What knowledge or behaviors need to shift?
What dependencies will be disrupted?
What processes need re-training or redesign?

Without this kind of analysis, change creates confusion, friction, and unnecessary resistance—even when the change itself is positive. The same is true in your personal life.

Impact is the full map of what this shift touches. Different types of change have different levels and shapes of impact:

1. Impact in Anticipated Change

When you're planning a change—like moving, starting a business, shifting careers, or pursuing a major goal—you evaluate the impact ahead of time. **Ask yourself:**

What will this change require of me emotionally, mentally, financially, and physically?
What routines will need to shift?
How will this affect the people around me?
What new habits or skills will I need?
What support will I require?

Anticipated change gives you the gift of foresight. You can prepare for the impact before the change arrives.

2. Impact in Unexpected Change

When a change catches you off-guard—like a layoff, an argument that shifts a relationship, an injury, a sudden financial disruption—you often feel the impact before you fully understand it. You feel the emotional reaction immediately, but the practical effects unfold gradually. **Ask yourself:**

What has already shifted in my day-to-day life?
What responsibilities, expectations, or routines are immediately affected?

What secondary effects am I beginning to feel?
What parts of my life feel unstable or uncertain?
What do I need to temporarily pause, adjust, or renegotiate?

Unexpected change requires patience. Impact reveals itself over time, not all at once.

3. Impact in Life-Altering Change

Some changes alter the shape of your world entirely—death, betrayal, illness, divorce, or a moment that changes the course of your identity. With these experiences, impact is multidimensional. It touches your beliefs, your sense of safety, your confidence, your relationships, and often your view of yourself. **Ask yourself:**

How has this changed what I expect of the world?
What feels different about how I see myself?
What parts of my identity feel shaken or redefined?
How has my capacity, energy, or perspective shifted?
What parts of my life are being rebuilt, not just adjusted?

Life-altering change has the widest reach, and understanding its impact brings compassion to the process of rebuilding.

Impact Is a Map

People often avoid examining impact because they fear they'll feel overwhelmed by what the change touches. But impact brings what is already happening into view so you can address it instead of being blindsided by it.

Impact doesn't ask, *"Why is this happening?"*
It asks, *"Where is this happening?"*

It maps the terrain—your routines, stability, relationships, responsibilities, and internal systems—so you understand the landscape you're moving through. When you see impact clearly, you stop expecting yourself to move at a pace or with a level of capacity that doesn't match your reality. You begin to make decisions that are aligned with the world you live in, not the one you wish you were in.

Illustrative Example
The Ripple Beneath the Surface

Imagine someone saying, "I'm thinking about moving to a new city." On the surface, it sounds like a simple change of location. But the moment they step into Impact, the fuller picture becomes unmistakable.

Emotionally, the move feels exciting but also uncertain. There's anticipation, but also the quiet fear of starting over. Socially, it means leaving behind a circle of friends, neighbors, and familiar routines that have anchored them. Financially, the shift may require adjusting to a new cost of living, saving for deposits, or preparing to sell their current home. Practically, the logistics multiply with finding a new property, preparing the old one for sale, learning new routes, choosing new childcare options, and adjusting to new daily rhythms.

Relationally, family dynamics shift as responsibilities are redistributed and everyone prepares for a new rhythm. Support systems evolve—some parts become less immediate, others newly available. Professionally, the move may involve a new role, a new team, or a shift in career trajectory, each with its unknowns. And quietly, identity is affected too; the person must reconcile who they've been in one place with who they will become in another.

None of these ripples are good or bad; they are simply real. And when the person can see them clearly, they can prepare for them rather than being blindsided by them. The move stops being just a relocation and becomes a transition they are equipped to navigate.

That is the purpose of understanding impact.

It arms you with awareness instead of anxiety.

It gives you foresight rather than fear.

And it ensures the next phase—**OWN**—is built on truth rather than assumptions.

Future State: Defining Direction and Identifying What Will Keep You Moving

If your current state reveals where you are, your future state reveals where you intend to go. It is the part of DISCOVER that brings direction to the journey, a clear sense of where you are moving and why it matters. People often skip this step because they mistake desire for direction. They say things like, "I just want to be happier," or "I want a better life," or "I want stability," without defining what those words mean in their specific context.

A future state is not a vague wish or an inspiring affirmation; it is a grounded intention. It is the destination you are steering toward, even if the path is not fully formed.

In organizational change, the future state is always defined before implementation begins. A company does not simply say, *"We want to be better."* They identify the specific outcomes: improved processes, clearer communication, increased efficiency, upgraded systems, enhanced customer experience. They articulate what "better" means so the organization can move in a unified direction. Without that clarity, departments drift, teams misalign, and everyone expends energy without making meaningful progress.

Your personal life operates the same way. It's not enough to know that you want something different; you need to understand what *different* means for you. But in personal change, there is another layer organizations define that most people completely overlook: your motivating factors.

> Motivating factors are the reasons the change matters to you—the "why" beneath the desire. They are the part of the process that connects the outcome you want to the person you are. And without them, personal change becomes fragile.

Motivating factors serve as the anchor when the journey becomes shaky or uncertain. They remind you why you started when you hit discomfort, doubt, or fatigue. They ground you on the days when the process feels slower than you expected, when fear shows up, or when the old way of doing things feels easier than the new one.

Most people lose momentum because they never identified what was fueling them in the first place. They set a goal without anchoring it to meaning. They chase an outcome without understanding the desire behind it. And when the emotional friction appears—as it always does—they assume they're failing rather than recognizing they were never anchored.

Motivating factors give the change direction. They create the emotional architecture that holds the process in place. They allow the work to feel purposeful rather than performative. And when you name them clearly, the process shifts from something you're forcing to something you're committed to.

Future State in Anticipated Change

When choosing a change intentionally, your future state is aspirational yet grounded. It gives you direction and helps you name what you're truly pursuing. **Ask yourself:**

What does "better" look like in specific terms?
How do I want to feel on the other side of this change?
What would success look like for me?
What meaningful difference do I want this change to make in my life?

Then identify your motivating factors:

Why do I want this change?

Why now?

What deeper need or value is this tied to?

How will this improve the quality of my life, my relationships, or my well-being?

When, not if, the excitement fades, your motivating factors become the fuel that keeps you moving.

Future State in Unexpected Change

When change arrives without warning, the future state shifts. You're not dreaming of something new; you're stabilizing something that has been disrupted. **Ask yourself:**

What do I need in order to feel grounded again?

What immediate outcomes would help me regain a sense of direction?

What small wins would help me stabilize and move forward?

Then identify motivating factors:

What am I protecting?

What am I rebuilding for?

What matters most to me in how I move through this?

Who or what do I want to show up well for?

These become your internal anchors as you adjust to the new reality.

Future State in Life

Life-altering change reshapes the future state entirely. You are now learning how to live in a world that now looks different. **Ask yourself:**

What would healing or steadying look like for me?
What do I need to regain a sense of self?
What aspects of my life need to be rebuilt, not just restored?
Then identify motivating factors with compassion:
What is giving me strength right now?
What do I want to reclaim in myself?
What values feel even more important after this change?
What future feels possible, even if I'm not ready to commit to it yet?

In life-altering change, motivating factors are lifelines.

Future State Is Orientation

Your future state gives you the desired direction you need so your next steps make sense. Without direction, change becomes a cycle of reacting instead of progressing.

And with motivating factors, your future state becomes something you can return to when your emotions fluctuate, when the path feels unclear, or when you doubt whether you're capable of continuing.

Motivating factors are the *why* behind the journey and support you through the discomfort that change inevitably brings.

Illustrative Example
When the Path Gets Shaky

Imagine someone preparing to go back to school as an adult. On the surface, their future state may sound simple: *"I want a better career."* But when they move through DISCOVER, the picture deepens.

Their true future state is:
"I want a career where I feel valued, challenged, and compensated in a way that supports my family."

Their motivating factors are:

I want to create stability for my children.
I want to break outdated narratives about what is possible for me.
I want to feel proud of the life I'm building.

Six months later, when the coursework becomes overwhelming or self-doubt creeps in, they don't continue because school is exciting; they continue because they are anchored to *why* the change matters.

Motivation rooted in meaning outlasts motivation rooted in momentum.

A grounded future state gives direction.
Clear motivating factors give endurance.

Together, they prepare you for the next phase—**OWN**—where you decide how you will show up for the journey ahead.

The Diagnostic You Can't Afford to Skip

DISCOVER is real work. It is the diagnostic stage of change, and there is a tremendous amount of learning that happens here. When you move too quickly past this phase, you're moving without the information you need. Skipping DISCOVER leads to making decisions without a true read on your reality. Without that understanding, you don't have true direction; you have guesses.

> Taking your time in DISCOVER informs your progress. The more honestly you see your current state, the impact of the change, and the future you're moving toward, the more grounded your next steps become. Without that, you begin to grasp at straws—chasing distractions, trying every possible solution, and feeling frustrated when nothing seems to work.

As you consider how you manage change right now, pause for a moment and reflect: How much DISCOVER have you actually done? How often do you move straight to action without truly understanding what's happening inside you? How often do you see this in the people around you, or in the way the world responds to disruption, rushing to solutions without fully naming the problem?

DISCOVER invites you to do it differently. It asks you to learn before you leap, to understand before you decide, and to see the landscape before you choose a path. And once you've done that, you're ready for the next phase: **OWN**, where you decide how you will respond in light of everything you've uncovered.

CHAPTER 4

OWN

The Shift From Reaction to Intention

After DISCOVER gives you the truth of where you are, OWN asks a new question: How will you choose to show up in light of everything you now know?

This is the phase where orientation becomes agency. It is where the emotional fog begins to settle, and where you reclaim the pen instead of letting the change write your story for you. Unlike the instinctual reactions that often arise when change arrives, such as panic, avoidance, over-functioning, freezing, Ownership is a conscious choice. People misunderstand ownership because they confuse it with blame or perfection. Ownership is not a moral evaluation. It is not holding yourself responsible for what happened, nor is it about being strong or certain or endlessly composed. Ownership is simply the practice of recognizing what is within your influence and what is not, and deciding how you will show up for both.

Ownership is the moment you shift from, *"This is happening to me,"* to, *"This is happening, and I get to choose how I move through it."*

It is not power over the situation; it is power within it.

True ownership is often misunderstood because the word itself has been diluted by self-help culture. People hear "take ownership" and assume it means carrying the burden alone, taking blame for everything, forcing a positive attitude, or pushing themselves to be strong. But that is pressure dressed up as responsibility.

> Ownership is clarity in motion—a grounded understanding of your internal and external reality, paired with the willingness to participate in your own transition.

It is the recognition that regardless of how a change entered your life, you are no longer a passive character in the story. You are an active one. Ownership is the moment you stop outsourcing your power to fear, circumstance, or other people's expectations. It is where you stop assuming that the change itself holds all the control, and begin to reclaim the parts that belong to you—your interpretation, posture, pace, boundaries, decisions, and next steps.

Ownership doesn't require confidence. It asks only one thing: that you show up with intention, even when you're unsure.

It is the internal equivalent of shifting from the passenger seat into the driver's seat. The terrain ahead may still be unpredictable, but you are no longer being carried by the momentum of the moment. You are guiding your experience through it and deciding when to accelerate, when to slow down, when to pause, and when to reroute.

But to understand ownership fully, it helps to distinguish it from what it is often mistaken for.

What We Mistake for Ownership

Blame

Blame collapses everything inward, convincing you that whatever happened is a direct reflection of your failures. It places the entire weight of the situation on your shoulders, even when the circumstances were shaped by many factors or never in your control. Blame shrinks your power because it prioritizes guilt over growth. That is not ownership. Ownership is not a judgment.

Control

Control tries to micromanage every detail, predict every outcome, and force life into a specific shape. It is rigid and exhausting, driven by the belief that if you tighten your grip enough, you can avoid discomfort or uncertainty. But control disconnects you from adaptability, which is the very thing change requires. Ownership, in contrast, lets you remain responsive without losing yourself.

Emotional Suppression

Convincing yourself to be "fine," unaffected, or endlessly stable only creates pressure. Suppression disconnects you from your needs, your signals, and your ability to self-regulate. Ownership doesn't ask you to mute anything; it asks you to understand your emotions so you can guide yourself through them.

Self-sacrifice

Taking everything on alone, absorbing everyone else's needs, or pushing through without rest is not ownership. Self-sacrifice teaches you to measure your worth by how much you can endure instead of how well you can care for yourself. Ownership does not require you to disappear to keep everything else standing.

Perfection

There is no flawless decision-making in change, no perfectly timed response, no ideal pace. Chasing perfection keeps you stuck in overthinking instead of moving forward. Ownership allows pauses, course corrections, and learning. Perfection does not.

In essence, ownership is not pressure.
It is not silence, strain, or a moral scorecard.
And it is not an invitation to carry more than you were meant to.

What True Ownership Looks Like

Ownership requires participation, your willingness to stay engaged in your transition rather than stepping back and letting the change drag you. It's an active stance, not a passive one. Even when the road is uneven or uncertain, Ownership is the decision to keep your hands on the wheel.

Step into radical self-honesty.

Ownership invites you to acknowledge your fears, limits, habits, patterns, and strengths without spiraling into shame or pretending they aren't there. It takes courage to look inward clearly and compassionately; forcing confidence is easy. Honesty is far more powerful.

Ownership is an intentional posture.

It is choosing how you want to show up internally before deciding what to do externally. It is the commitment to respond from alignment rather than panic, defensiveness, or conditioning. It is the shift from, *"This is happening to me,"* to, *"This is happening and I choose how I move within it."*

Ownership offers alignment.

Ownership means making choices that match your values, goals, and capacity instead of following ones driven by fear, urgency, people-pleasing, or old survival strategies. It is movement that reflects the person you are becoming, not the patterns you've outgrown.

And ownership is adaptability.

Even the best plans meet unexpected turns. Something will shift. A new variable will appear. A step you trusted may fall through. Ownership gives you permission to adjust, to revisit DISCOVER if the landscape changes, and to stay engaged without collapsing.

Above all, Ownership is self-leadership.

It is the decision to guide yourself through uncertainty rather than abandon yourself to the moment. It is showing up with intention even on the days you don't yet feel confident. It is choosing your direction, your values, and your growth—again and again, one grounded choice at a time.

A Visual: Misperceptions vs. True Ownership

Common Misperceptions of Ownership

(what people think ownership requires)

- Taking blame

- Pushing through without rest

- Hiding emotions

- Controlling every outcome

- Doing everything alone

- Acting confident

- Perfection or flawless decision-making

- Never wavering or doubting
- "If it goes wrong, it's my fault."

True Ownership

(what ownership actually is)

- Acknowledging reality honestly
- Choosing your posture intentionally
- Identifying what is and isn't in your control
- Staying engaged in your OWN process
- Allowing help and support
- Regulating yourself enough to make grounded choices
- Adapting when new information arises
- Aligning actions with values, not fear
- "Even if it's hard, I won't abandon myself."

Understanding what ownership is—and what it is not—creates the foundation for the next layer of this phase: your mindset. Ownership may be the posture you hold in relation to the change, but mindset is the internal environment that makes that posture possible. If ownership is the vehicle that carries you through the transition, mindset is the operating system running quietly underneath every thought, interpretation, and decision you make. Without a grounded mindset, ownership becomes difficult to sustain because without ownership, mindset has nowhere to go. They work together, shaping how you move through the change long before you take a single action in the IMPLEMENT phase.

Mindset: The Internal System That Shapes How You Experience Change

Before ownership becomes action, it begins as mindset. And mindset, despite how casually the word gets used in personal development spaces, is not about staying positive or repeating affirmations until life shifts. It's an internal operating system: the beliefs, interpretations, and mental habits that shape how you understand what's happening to you. It influences how your brain processes uncertainty, how your nervous system responds to stress, and how your body mobilizes or shuts down when life changes.

When a change occurs, even one you actively choose, the brain makes an immediate assessment: *Is this safe or is this a threat?* This evaluation is an unconscious, ancient survival mechanism wired into the human nervous system. The brain is designed to prioritize predictability because predictability signals safety. Change disrupts that safety, so the brain often interprets the shift as potential danger long before you have time to logically process what is unfolding. This is where mindset begins its work.

> Mindset influences how the brain labels the change, and that label determines which parts of the brain become dominant.

If your mindset interprets the change as catastrophic, permanent, or personal, your nervous system shifts into a threat state. Heart rate increases, breathing becomes shallow, the chest tightens, and cortisol rises. The amygdala takes the lead while the prefrontal cortex—the part of the brain you need most during change—moves to the background. You may feel overwhelmed, foggy, reactive, or frozen, because your brain is trying, quite literally, to protect you.

A grounded mindset produces a different internal pattern. It acknowledges discomfort without catastrophizing it. It allows you to feel what you feel while reminding your brain that the situation, however difficult, is navigable. This interpretation calms the nervous system enough to keep the prefrontal cortex online. You can think more clearly, regulate more effectively, and choose more intentionally. A grounded approach ensures that your internal system doesn't shut down in response to the change.

In other words, mindset helps keep your brain available to you. This is why grounding techniques, mindfulness practices, and therapeutic breathing strategies create immediate relief. They aren't "soft skills" or spiritual add-ons; they are neurological interventions. When you slow your breath or orient yourself to the present moment, you reduce amygdala activation—the brain's fear and alarm center—and re-engage the prefrontal cortex, which handles planning, reasoning, and perspective.

These signals tell your nervous system, *"I am safe enough to stay engaged."* Once the internal alarm lowers, higher-level thinking becomes accessible again.

For me, this often looks simple and practical: I ground myself by orienting my senses by naming five things I can see, four I can hear, three I can touch, and so on. It takes less than a minute, and it reliably shifts my brain out of threat mode and back into awareness, where clear thinking and intentional choice become possible again.

From a psychological perspective, mindset is a set of cognitive frames, think mental lenses that shape how you interpret what's happening. These frames influence whether a change feels catastrophic or manageable, permanent or temporary, defining or informative. Mindset determines the meaning you assign to the disruption. And meaning determines behavior. If you interpret a setback as evidence that you are falling apart, you will act accordingly. If you interpret it as part of your evolution, your behavior shifts toward resilience, adaptability, and growth.

What makes mindset even more influential is the way it interacts with the body. Thoughts don't stay in your head; they create biochemical responses throughout your entire system. A single fearful thought can shift your breathing, posture, digestion, energy, and emotional bandwidth. When those thoughts become habitual, the nervous system can remain in a prolonged state of activation, making it harder to access creativity, problem-solving, and emotional regulation—all essential during change.

A grounded mindset, by contrast, supports what psychologists call adaptive regulation: the ability to respond to stress without being overtaken by it. When your mindset is steady, your body interprets the change as a challenge it can navigate rather than a threat it must escape. This doesn't eliminate discomfort, but it prevents discomfort from spiraling into panic or paralysis.

> Mindset helps you interpret reality in a way that keeps you capable.

This is where DISCOVER and mindset intersect. The mindset you bring into OWN is more informed. When you understand your current state, you know the emotional and practical weight you're carrying. When you understand the impact, you see which parts of your life are stretching or shifting. When you define your future state and identify your motivating factors, your brain has direction and purpose, the two elements proven to reduce the stress response and increase resilience.

DISCOVER gives your brain context.
Mindset gives your brain coherence.

Together, they create an internal environment that supports stability rather than reactivity. You don't have to feel courageous or confident to have a grounded mindset. You simply have to be willing to guide your internal dialogue with honesty rather than fear. This does not mean telling yourself the situation is easy or pretending you're unaffected. It means reminding yourself that you still have choice and influence. Mindset is the internal orientation that makes choice possible.

Once mindset is grounded, ownership becomes more of a practice. And this leads to the next part: how mindset translates into the actual choices that shape your experience of change.

The Choice That Changes Everything

Choice is the hinge between your internal world and your external actions. It is the point where understanding becomes direction. People often assume choice is obvious such as, "I can choose how I respond." But during change, especially when emotions are heightened and the nervous system is activated, choice becomes more complex and more significant than simply deciding what to do next.

> Choice in the context of change is not about selecting an outcome; it is about selecting a stance. It is the moment you decide whether you will move through the transition reactively or intentionally.

A reactive stance is driven by old patterns, survival instincts, and unchecked narratives. An intentional stance is guided by your grounded mindset, your motivating factors, and the truth you uncovered in DISCOVER.

From a psychological perspective, this is the moment you interrupt automatic behaviors. The brain loves predictability, and when confronted with uncertainty, it defaults to familiar patterns—shutting down, over functioning, withdrawing, pleasing, pushing harder, or avoiding entirely. These patterns aren't reflections of character; they are reflections of conditioning. They are learned responses the brain uses to manage discomfort, shortcuts it believes will keep you safe in the short term, even if they cost you alignment in the long term.

Choice breaks the automatic loop.

When you consciously choose your stance, you activate regions of the brain associated with executive functioning—planning, reflection, judgment, and self-regulation. Instead of reverting to instinctual responses from the amygdala (fear and survival), you bring your prefrontal cortex back into leadership. This shift is subtle but profound. You create space between stimulus and response, allowing yourself to engage with the situation instead of being swept away by it. Those few seconds where you pause, breathe, and decide is where ownership starts to move from theory into lived practice.

Choice sounds like this internally:
"I acknowledge how I feel, and I will not let this feeling dictate my next step."
"I can't control what happened, but I can influence what I do now."
"I can move slowly without being stuck."
"I can be afraid and still choose what supports me."

This is psychological flexibility, the ability to hold discomfort in one hand and agency in the other.

Choice also requires honesty. You cannot choose well if you are pretending the change is easier than it is or if you deny the emotional reality of your experience. That is why DISCOVER precedes this stage; it gives you the full picture so your choices are rooted in truth rather than avoidance or overconfidence. Mindset then interprets that truth in a way that keeps your brain and body available to you, so when it is time to choose, you choose from grounded awareness.

In anticipated change, choice looks like committing to the habits, boundaries, and behaviors that support the life you say you want.

In unexpected change, choice looks like stabilizing your emotions long enough to respond rather than react.

In life-altering change, choice looks like gentleness with yourself and the decision to keep moving—even if the steps are small or uneven.

What many people don't realize is that every choice you make during change, even the smallest ones, begin to reshape your identity. You reinforce to your brain, "I can trust myself here. I can move through this. I can handle uncertainty." These micro-reinforcements accumulate, gradually shifting your self-perception from someone change happens to into someone who moves through change with intention.

Over time, the brain lays down new pathways: instead of defaulting to shutdown, it begins to default to, *"Pause. Breathe. Choose."* That is how identity shifts to a series of moments where you choose differently than you used to.

This is what makes choice transformative. It isn't built in big moments, but in consistent alignment between your internal posture and your outward behavior.

Choice is the moment you decide: "I cannot control everything in this situation, but I choose how I engage."

This sets the stage for the next phase—IMPLEMENT—where choices become action, and movement becomes the teacher that reveals what the path ahead actually requires.

Illustrative Mindset Examples

(Same situation, different internal experience)

To really understand mindset, it helps to see it in motion as an internal experience that changes everything around the same event. These examples also show how mindset shapes how you feel and which choices you even recognize as available. Let's look at a few real-world situations:

Example 1. The Layoff

The external event is the same:
You receive an email from HR asking you to join a "quick meeting," and within fifteen minutes, you learn your role has been eliminated.

Nothing about the logistics changes between one version of this moment and another. The news is the same. The timing is the same. What changes is the mindset interpreting it.

Reactive, threat-based mindset:
In this frame, the brain categorizes the layoff as proof of personal failure and long-term catastrophe. The internal dialogue sounds like:

"This means I wasn't good enough."

"No one else will hire me."

"I've ruined everything."

Biologically, this mindset keeps the nervous system in a state of heightened alarm. Breathing becomes shallow, thoughts race, the body tightens. The future collapses into a singular narrative: "This is the beginning of the end." In this state, the prefrontal cortex—the part of the brain that plans, problem-solves, and assesses options—is pushed to the background while fear and shame take the lead. Action, if taken at all, tends to be frantic, avoidant, or shut down.

Grounded, challenge-focused mindset:
In this frame, the brain still registers a shock, but the meaning assigned to the event shifts. The internal dialogue sounds more like:

"This is a serious disruption, and I'm allowed to feel that."

"This doesn't erase my skills or my worth."

"I will need time and support, but I can figure out my next step."

Here, the layoff is still painful and unwelcome, but the mind holds onto possibility. The nervous system is activated, yes, but not abandoned. Breath can be brought back under control. The person may text a friend, take a walk, or calmly review their severance paperwork rather than spiraling into self-condemnation.

The prefrontal cortex stays more available, which means they can evaluate options, think about contacts, review finances, and create a draft plan, even if it's a rough one.

The event is the same.
The biology is the same.
The mindset is different.
And because the mindset is different, the entire internal experience and the next set of choices changes.

2. *The Relationship Conversation*

The external event:
Your partner says, "I feel like we haven't really been connecting lately, and I'm not happy with how we've been communicating."

Same words. Same moment. Same living room.
But mindset splits the experience in two entirely different directions.

Defensive, self-protective mindset:
In this frame, the feedback is processed as accusation. The mind hears: "You're failing. You're the problem." The inner voice quickly translates the comment into global, self-critical conclusions:
"I'm a terrible partner."
"Nothing I do is ever enough."

The body responds accordingly as the heart rate increases, shoulders tense, and jaw tightens. The nervous system prepares for attack or retreat. In this state, listening becomes nearly impossible. The person may shut down, lash out, deflect, or flip the conversation to the partner's flaws. Connection—the very thing being asked for—becomes further out of reach.

Curious, connection-focused mindset:
The words are the same, but the internal lens shifts. The brain still feels exposed because no one loves hearing that their partner is unhappy, but curiosity softens the edges. The inner dialogue sounds more like:

"This is hard to hear, but they're sharing this because they want something to improve."

"I may not agree with everything, but I want to understand."

"This doesn't mean I'm a failure; it means there's something we need to work on."

The nervous system still notices the discomfort, yet the person consciously brings their body into regulation by slowing their breathing, relaxing their shoulders, making eye contact. This keeps the prefrontal cortex engaged and allows for questions like:

"Can you tell me more about what hasn't felt good?"

"When do you feel most disconnected?"

One mindset turns the moment into evidence of unworthiness. The other turns it into an entry point for deeper connection.

3. The Personal Goal: Going Back to School Later in Life

The external event:
You're considering enrolling in a program to pursue a credential or degree you didn't complete earlier in your life.

Nothing about the brochures, tuition numbers, or application deadlines changes between one mindset and another, but the internal experience does.

Fixed, self-limiting mindset:

The narrative, often rooted in older experiences and internalized messages, sounds like:

"I should have done this years ago; it's too late now."

"Everyone else will be younger and more capable."

"If I start and struggle, it will just prove I wasn't cut out for this."

The brain sorts the idea into the "risk of exposure" category. The body responds with tension; the nervous system anticipates embarrassment or failure. From that state, avoidance feels protective. The person may decide, "It's easier not to try," framing that choice as practicality when it is, in reality, fear reinforced by mindset.

Growth-oriented, self-honoring mindset:

Here, the person still recognizes the challenge:

"This will stretch me, and it might be hard."

But they pair that truth with another:

"I'm allowed to invest in myself at this stage."

"My experience is an asset, not a defect."

"If I struggle, it means I'm learning."

The nervous system still feels the flutter of uncertainty, but the brain has a different story to pair it with—one that doesn't interpret discomfort as a sign to stop. From this mindset, the person might attend an information session, email an advisor, or begin with one class rather than a full course load. The external circumstances are unchanged. The internal posture is not.

What These Examples Really Show

In each scenario, the situation stays exactly the same. What shifts is:

- the meaning assigned to the event,
- the way the nervous system responds,
- which parts of the brain are most active, and
- the types of choices that become available.

This is mindset in action, guiding what your brain does with the reality in front of you so your body can support you instead of sabotage you—and so your choices reflect your values instead of your fears.

When you understand that mindset shapes your entire internal experience of the same external event, ownership stops sounding like a motivational slogan and becomes what it truly is: a deliberate decision about how you will relate to the change you're in.

And once that decision is made, your next move becomes clearer. Chapter 5 begins there, where intention turns into action, one aligned step at a time.

Chapter 5

IMPLEMENT

The Shift From Preparation to Participation

Implementation is the moment when change leaves the inner world and enters the outer one. Up to this point, everything has been happening inside you—your understanding, awareness, grounding, and agency. DISCOVER helped you see the truth of where you are and what has shifted. OWN helped you reclaim your posture, mindset, and ability to navigate the emotional terrain ahead of you. But insight alone, no matter how deep, cannot create movement. Transformation only happens when you act in accordance with that understanding.

This is where many people freeze. They assume implementation requires certainty, confidence, or perfection. They imagine that the next step must be the correct one, or that they must map out the entire journey before they take their first action. But change does not bend to perfection. Change responds to participation.

> Implementation is not a performance or a demonstration of readiness or mastery. It is the willingness to begin before you feel complete, the courage to take a step before you know exactly where it will lead, and the trust that forward movement is what illuminates the path ahead.

The beginning may not feel triumphant. It rarely feels cinematic or bold. It often feels small, tentative, and unremarkable. Yet it is in this very ordinariness that the power of implementation lives. Beginning interrupts the inertia that holds people in cycles of thinking, preparing, hesitating, and analyzing. Beginning shifts you from internal possibility into external reality. It signals to your mind and body that you are no longer rehearsing your change—you are participating in it.

And once you participate, the landscape shifts. What was once blurry becomes slightly clearer, and what felt overwhelming becomes more defined. What appears impossible begins to break into parts that your brain can actually engage with. You discover that you do not need to see the entire road to take one meaningful step. Implementation, in its truest form, teaches you that movement reveals what contemplation cannot.

To fully understand this, it helps to begin with a more honest picture of what progress looks like, a picture that reflects your humanity.

A Metaphor for Implementing Change: The River With Bends

People often imagine progress as a straight line, stretching neatly from where they are to where they want to be. It is an appealing idea, especially for high-functioning, goal-oriented individuals who take pride in efficiency and directness. But progress—real, enduring progress—does not move in clean, geometric patterns. Nothing else in nature moves that way, and neither do human beings.

A more accurate image is a river.

A river never moves in a straight, uninterrupted course. It curves, bends, widens, narrows, speeds up, slows down, and shifts its shape in response to the terrain it encounters. From above, the river's path can look erratic, even inefficient. But from within, each bend serves a purpose. The river adapts because adaptation is what allows it to continue moving. It adjusts to rocks, pressure, depth, resistance, and opportunity. It flows around obstacles rather than stopping at them.

This is precisely how implementation unfolds.

When you take a step toward change, the terrain shifts as new information appears and unexpected emotions surface. Responsibilities, needs, or limitations you weren't aware of make themselves known. You find yourself curving because the path requires it. You slow down at moments when the emotional demands of life require steadiness rather than acceleration. You pause because your mind and body need space to catch up. You adapt, just as the river does, to the realities of your landscape.

These bends are not setbacks. They are the shape of progress.

The river never doubts itself because it curves. It curves because that is how it keeps moving forward. In the same way, your IMPLEMENTation may not look linear, predictable, or efficient. But each turn, each correction, each pause, each acceleration holds meaning. When you allow yourself to move with the change rather than against it, you discover that progress is defined by continuity.

Implementation is learning to trust the bends.

Movement Is the Teacher

One of the biggest misconceptions people carry into change is the belief that clarity must precede action. It is a comforting idea that once you know exactly what to do, you will finally take the step. But clarity is not a prerequisite for movement. In practice, clarity is a result of movement. The insights that feel unreachable from the safety of your thoughts often become obvious after you act. Movement exposes what planning cannot, revealing what you genuinely want, what you are ready for, what you thought you wanted but don't, and what needs more time, support, or refinement.

In organizational change management, this principle is foundational. No major initiative is implemented in one sweeping motion. Companies test and pilot by gathering feedback and running phased rollouts. They refine their strategy in real-time based on the behaviors, reactions, and needs that emerge. The plan evolves because the organization learns more by doing than by projecting.

Individuals are no different.

People often believe that thinking about change is the same as preparing for change. But thinking is only one form of preparation—and often, an incomplete one. Real preparation happens in motion, such as when you take a step and evaluate what it gives back to you. It happens when you test your assumptions and learn which ones hold true. It happens when you engage with your environment, your goals, and your emotional landscape, allowing the experience itself to refine your direction.

When that happens, movement teaches. It provides feedback. It reveals misalignment and clarifies what fits. It transforms abstract desires into embodied experiences. You learn your capacity by stretching it, your preferences by exercising them, your patterns by activating them, and your resilience by watching yourself move through what once felt overwhelming.

People often underestimate how much information they receive simply by beginning.

A step that feels energizing tells you something valuable. A step that drains you tells you something equally meaningful. A step that feels confusing may indicate that you need a different entry point. A step that feels steady confirms that you are moving in alignment with both your current reality and your future direction.

None of this information is accessible until you move. Implementation asks you to participate in the act of movement. It trusts that the act of moving reveals what contemplation cannot.

Small Steps Are Strategic

If movement is the teacher, then small steps are the language that makes learning accessible. People often underestimate small steps because they assume meaningful progress must be dramatic—sweeping decisions, bold declarations, or large, disruptive action. They imagine the shift between one life and the next must be unmistakable enough to announce itself.

Sustainable change rarely begins that way. The pressure to create big movement is often what stops people from moving at all. When someone believes action must be intense to matter, they conclude that if they cannot leap, they shouldn't step. This belief has silently stalled more transformations than any external barrier ever could.

Small steps are not placeholders for real action.

Small steps *are* real action.

From a psychological standpoint, small steps are the most effective path to change because they work with the brain rather than against it. The human nervous system is built to detect threats, and sweeping change often triggers protective responses like avoidance, anxiety, shut down, and overwhelm. Small steps bypass the alarm system. They signal safety, manageability, and control. They create a rhythm your system can adapt to rather than a disruption it must brace against.

This is why a single small action can have a disproportionate impact. It shifts your physiology. It alters your emotional state. It gives your brain something it cannot create through thinking alone: proof that you can move, begin, stay intact, and act even when uncertain.

> Small steps help generate self-trust. You trust that you will follow through. You trust you can handle discomfort. You trust you can adjust. Self-trust is not built through dramatic leaps; it is built through consistent evidence that you do not abandon yourself in motion.

You can see this clearly in the world of health and dieting. Extreme diets often fail because the body interprets abrupt restriction as a threat. The nervous system pushes back, so willpower collapses. One disrupted day becomes a spiral of self-blame. The change was too big and too disconnected from real life to be sustainable. But small, consistent shifts—one nourishing habit, one improved meal, or one short walk—do not trigger alarm. Habits stack quietly. Confidence grows. Identity shifts from "trying to be healthy" to "being someone who makes healthy choices."

Lifestyle changes can then succeed because they honor the brain's need for safety and gradual adaptation.

Small steps also generate information without requiring perfection and invite curiosity. They help you test assumptions, reveal misalignment, and uncover emotional or logistical realities no amount of planning could predict.

Small steps gently correct your course as you move, and they allow you to adjust before you've invested so much energy that you feel trapped. They refine your direction through real feedback instead of hopeful forecasting.

When people rush into big steps just so they can feel like they're "finally doing something," they pour out energy without gathering clarity. They exhaust themselves and interpret the exhaustion as failure. But the issue isn't ability—it's scale. They tried to sprint through the learning curve and collapsed under the speed.

Small steps honor your humanity.

They respect your emotional bandwidth.

They account for your nervous system.

They leave room for your responsibilities.

They adapt to your reality rather than trying to override it.

Most importantly, small steps keep you in the process.

In other words, when the change is too big, you step out. When the change is manageable, you stay engaged. And engagement is the true engine of transformation. Big steps create movement; small steps create momentum.

Small steps also lower emotional friction. Big actions require ideal alignment of confidence, energy, timing, and capacity, while small actions require only enough willingness for this moment. They lower the bar for participation without reducing the impact. This reduces psychological resistance, increases follow-through, and preserves energy for the next step.

Another reason small steps matter: they give your identity room to evolve. When you force yourself into a version of your future you haven't grown into yet, the dissonance becomes unbearable. You retreat because the leap demanded an identity you haven't built yet. Identity evolves through repetition, the steady rhythm of action that teaches you who you are becoming.

And once enough small steps accumulate, you realize something profound: you did not transform through one dramatic moment—you transformed through the subtle, steady build of consistent action. Small steps are not what you do when the big step feels out of reach; they are the architecture of lasting change.

Implementation begins with movement.

Momentum is built through small steps.

And durable change is created through consistency.

Action Aligned With Your Capacity

Every change requires energy—emotional, mental, physical, and logistical. When people imagine implementing change, they tend to imagine action without accounting for the capacity that must sustain it. They picture themselves moving at full speed, fueled by inspiration, clarity, or determination. But real change, especially meaningful, lasting change, cannot rely on adrenaline. It must rely on alignment, which is only possible when you understand your true capacity, not the version of capacity you wish you had.

Capacity is dynamic. It shifts with your circumstances, your responsibilities, your psychological load, your emotional bandwidth, and the season of life you are in. What you can carry on a calm week is not the same as what you can carry during a crisis. What you can hold when you are well-rested is not the same as what you can hold when your nervous system is taxed. Capacity reflects your internal and external conditions. Treating capacity as a fixed trait is one of the most common ways people unintentionally sabotage their progress.

This misunderstanding is not unique to individuals. In organizational change management, capacity is a core consideration. Leaders examine workloads, resource constraints, competing priorities, and the emotional climate of their teams before launching any significant initiative. They understand that people have finite bandwidth. They stagger timelines, build support structures, and adjust expectations. They do not measure commitment by how much someone can take on; instead, they measure readiness by how much the system can sustain. When organizations ignore capacity, projects collapse. Not because the goals were flawed, but because the load exceeded the system's ability to carry it.

Yet individuals often hold themselves to far harsher standards than any effective leader would impose on a team. They pressure themselves to take massive steps even when their energy is depleted. They push themselves to IMPLEMENT change at a pace that does not match their emotional or logistical reality. They treat exhaustion as a personal failure. They treat lack of capacity as a character flaw rather than an environmental truth. They imagine that discipline should override depletion, and that "powering through" is evidence of strength.

But change implemented from depletion is fragile and collapses under the weight of the demands it creates. Implementation done without regard for capacity leads to burnout, inconsistency, self-blame, and the quiet conclusion that "I guess I can't do this." That conclusion is almost never true. What is true is that the approach was unsustainable.

Action aligned with capacity, on the other hand, creates longevity. It honors both ambition and the nervous system. It respects both the desire for progress and the reality of what you can hold right now. It allows movement to remain steady rather than sporadic. It brings integrity to the process because you are no longer asking yourself to live at odds with what your body, mind, and life are capable of supporting.

Capacity-aligned action is not a reduction of effort. It is an elevation of wisdom. It begins with telling yourself the truth:

What am I actually able to carry today?
What emotional weight am I holding?
What mental load am I processing?
What responsibilities surround me?
What is realistic for the season I'm in?
What pace matches both my present and my aspirations?

When you answer these questions honestly, you begin to see that implementation is about ensuring the step you take today is one you can take again tomorrow—not in intensity, but in spirit. It is matching your movement to your availability so that your change becomes something you participate in consistently rather than something you attempt intensely and abandon quickly.

Action aligned with capacity changes the emotional experience of implementation. Instead of feeling like you're constantly behind, you feel supported by your decisions, and instead of feeling overwhelmed, you experience clarity. Instead of interpreting adjustment as failure, you understand it as calibration, and you settle into a rhythm that moves with your life rather than against it.

People often believe they are unmotivated when the truth is they are overwhelmed. They believe they are inconsistent when the truth is they are overextended. They believe they lack discipline when the truth is they lack capacity.

Action aligned with capacity removes these false narratives. It puts you back into partnership with yourself. It allows you to build momentum at the pace that belongs to you—not the pace that belongs to someone whose life, emotional landscape, or responsibilities look nothing like yours.

When you begin implementing from your actual capacity, you learn that progress does not require intensity. It requires continuation. You learn that you do not need to be powerful to take a step—you simply need to be present. You also learn that when you honor what you can hold, the path remains accessible. You stay engaged, grounded, and consistent, ultimately building momentum.

Letting Action Clarify, Correct, and Redirect

One of the most liberating truths about implementation is that your first step does not need to be your final one. People place immense pressure on the earliest stages of change, expecting themselves to predict outcomes, foresee obstacles, and select the perfect direction before they move. But implementation is a process of learning in motion. It is a practice of letting action illuminate what thinking alone cannot reach.

Every step you take is a source of information.

Some steps affirm your direction.

Some reveal a necessary adjustment.

Some uncover an emotional need you did not recognize before.

Some surface limitations you must account for.

Some highlight capacities you didn't know you had.

This information is not evidence that you miscalculated. It is evidence that you are learning. The purpose of implementation is to DISCOVER. When you move, you begin to understand which assumptions were accurate and which ones need to be reshaped. You begin to see the difference between what you thought you wanted and what actually aligns with who you are becoming. You uncover practical patterns, emotional triggers, and environmental influences that were invisible until movement brought them forward.

In organizational change, leaders understand this intimately. They build adjustment into the process. They expect to refine timelines, reallocate resources, update communication strategies, and redirect teams based on what emerges during implementation. No organization interprets course correction as failure. They interpret it as responsiveness, evidence that they are adapting to real data rather than clinging to an idealized plan.

Individuals, however, often interpret correction as a personal flaw. They assume they should have known better and that changing direction means they were unprepared. They assume the need to adjust means they are incapable or that every deviation is a setback instead of a continuation.

In truth, correction is not a sign of weakness; it is a sign of alignment. It means you are responding to what is actually happening, not to the imagined version of the change you created before you began. It means your self-awareness is active. It means your sense of direction is maturing. It means you are participating responsibly in your transformation rather than forcing yourself down a path that no longer fits.

> Correction is refinement and a natural, intelligent part of change.

It is also essential for your nervous system. When you permit yourself to adjust without self-judgment, you reduce the emotional friction associated with taking risks. You teach your brain that movement is safe, even when movement requires recalibration. You sustain your capacity by allowing your path to evolve, which in turn keeps you engaged with the process rather than retreating out of shame or overwhelm.

One of the most helpful truths to internalize is this: no step is wasted. Even the steps you reverse or redirect carry value. They show you what does not align, surfacing patterns you need to interrupt, clarifying needs you overlooked, and revealing the emotional realities beneath your goals. They also help you distinguish between dreams rooted in intuition and dreams rooted in external pressure. Most importantly, they deepen your understanding of yourself and your life.

Action invites correction.

Correction invites clarity.

Clarity invites deeper alignment.

Alignment invites momentum.

Each part strengthens the next.

This is why implementation requires humility, an openness to being surprised by yourself, an acceptance that your first assumptions may not hold, and a willingness to let reality shape your movement. It requires emotional flexibility, the capacity to shift without collapsing, and the discipline of staying engaged even when your path requires adjustment. Flexibility is a strategy. It is how you avoid hardening into a version of the plan you created before you understood its impact. It is how you remain open to the version of your future that emerges only after you begin walking toward it.

The most grounded implementers—the ones who sustain change rather than burning out—possess a quiet comfort with recalibration. They understand that progress rarely moves in a straight, predictable line. Progress moves with curiosity and allows steps to be teachers rather than tests while trusting that every correction is a form of intelligence that keeps them aligned with what truly matters.

> Implementation is not the art of moving perfectly. It is the art of moving, noticing, and adjusting.

This responsiveness is what makes implementation durable. It allows your change to breathe. It protects you from the rigidity that forces people into exhaustion and gives you permission to evolve as you learn. And it ensures that your path, however winding, remains yours.

Remember, a river doesn't move in a straight line; it moves in alignment with the landscape it's flowing through.

Your implementation works the same way. It shifts because movement brings the real path into view. When you let your actions guide and refine you, your direction becomes clearer, steadier, and more aligned with your future.

Implementation Across Anticipated, Unexpected, and Life-Altering Change

Although the mechanics of implementation remain consistent—movement, correction, capacity, and refinement—the emotional landscape shifts depending on the type of change you are navigating. What it takes to IMPLEMENT during a planned transition differs from what it takes during an unexpected disruption or a life-altering event. Understanding these differences allows you to meet yourself with accuracy and compassion rather than judgment or unrealistic expectations.

Implementation in Anticipated Change

Anticipated change often comes with hope, excitement, or intentional planning, and yet implementation in this category still requires steady, grounded action. Even when you want the change—whether it's a move, a career shift, a new relationship, or a personal goal—you will encounter moments where the reality of the transition challenges the fantasy of it. Enthusiasm does not eliminate complexity. Preparation does not eliminate uncertainty. Desire does not eliminate the need for discipline.

In anticipated change, implementation becomes the practice of translating aspiration into behavior. It is where the future you envisioned meets the realities of your daily life. The steps may feel more energizing because the destination is something you chose, but even chosen change introduces new demands. It requires the same principles: begin with what you can carry, take small steps that allow you to integrate the shift into your routine, and allow each step to refine your direction.

Action here often feels like activation. It is where excitement becomes structure, where intention becomes momentum. The emotional challenge is not the shock of the change but the patience required to build it. Many people underestimate how quickly inspiration fades once implementation begins. They confuse the high of envisioning the future with the stamina required to create it. The discipline of anticipated change becomes consistent. Implementation becomes the bridge between who you are and who you are choosing to become.

Implementation in Unexpected Change

Unexpected change is far less forgiving. It arrives without warning, disrupts your emotional equilibrium, and demands action before you feel ready. In these moments, implementation becomes less about building something new and more about stabilizing what exists. It is not about leaping forward; it is about finding your footing so you can eventually move with intention.

The first steps in unexpected change are often modest. They focus on safety, grounding, and delegation. You may need to regulate your emotions before you can make a rational decision. You may need to simplify your responsibilities before you can take on anything new. Implementation here is about responding, not performing. It is about making choices that protect your capacity while giving you enough structure to prevent you from spiraling into chaos.

In unexpected change, movement carries a different emotional texture. There is grief, shock, or disorientation woven into each step. Your nervous system may be on high alert. Your mind may race. You may feel suspended between what was and what is unfolding. IMPLEMENT honors this by asking for gentleness in your pacing. The goal is not rapid progress; the goal is stabilization. Once stabilized, you regain access to the deeper, more strategic parts of yourself, and from there, implementation begins to pick up its natural rhythm again.

Unexpected change reminds you that action does not need to be dramatic to be effective. Sometimes the most powerful step you can take is a small one that prevents you from retreating completely. Sometimes the victory is simply not abandoning yourself in the midst of the storm.

Implementation in Life-Altering Change

There are moments when change also asks you to reorient. In these seasons, the goal isn't advancement but finding yourself again. Implementation becomes less about forward progress and more about reconnecting to your internal bearings after the landscape of your life has shifted beneath you.

In life-altering change, implementation is measured in reentry. It is the gentle reintroduction of movement into a life that has been destabilized. The steps may be microscopic, such as making a phone call, attending one appointment, cleaning a corner of a room, eating a meal, getting out of bed, or stepping outside for a few minutes. These are small, powerful steps because your system is healing. This type of change requires an understanding of the body's need for safety, pacing, and restoration.

Here, movement becomes an act of resilience. Each action, no matter how modest, acknowledges that while everything around you has shifted, you are still capable of participating in your life. Every small step helps stitch together a sense of normalcy. Every gesture of engagement reminds you that you remain present, connected, and capable of influencing your experience, even when capacity fluctuates.

This category of change is where grace is essential. Implementation becomes less about pursuing a goal and more about slowly returning to yourself. You're not rebuilding a future yet; you're rebuilding the foundation a future can rest on. And here, the same truth still applies: movement matters. Even the smallest steps begin to stitch meaning back into your life. Gentle participation creates capacity, and with time, those small movements start opening space for what's next.

Yet across all forms of change, one principle remains constant: movement creates momentum. And as you continue to participate, whether your steps are quiet or confident, that momentum begins to take shape.

How Movement Becomes Momentum

Momentum is essentially your pace shifting. In the beginning, every step requires deliberate effort, much like the first days back in the gym when your body hasn't yet remembered what strength feels like. But as you repeat the movement, your system begins to adapt. Your muscles respond, your breathing steadies, and what once felt strenuous becomes familiar. The same thing happens internally during change. Momentum is your physiological and psychological adjustment to repeated action. With each step, your nervous system stops bracing against the unfamiliar and starts supporting your movement instead. The resistance decreases, the effort becomes more manageable, and your body and mind begin to work with you rather than against you.

Momentum grows quietly and builds when consistent steps start requiring less internal negotiation. The actions that once felt heavy or uncertain begin to settle into a rhythm. You no longer have to convince yourself to begin; beginning becomes part of how you move. What started as a deliberate effort shifts into something steadier and more natural. There is neuroscience behind this shift. Repetition teaches the brain that movement is safe. Neural pathways that support action become stronger, reducing the intensity of the fear response. Emotional friction decreases, and your tolerance for discomfort expands. As the change becomes familiar, your nervous system begins to regulate more easily because familiarity is one of its most powerful stabilizers.

As momentum forms, your relationship to obstacles begins to change. Without momentum, a setback feels like proof that you should stop or that you were never capable. But when you have a rhythm, obstacles become manageable. They are frustrations, not failures. Instead of stopping your movement, they require you to adjust your pace, explore another angle, or take a breath before continuing.

Momentum also influences identity. The more consistently you move, the more evidence you gather about who you are becoming. You start seeing yourself as someone who follows through, someone who adapts, someone who keeps going even without perfect conditions. This identity shift is earned. Your brain internalizes the repeated experience of action, and that lived evidence becomes the foundation for confidence. You no longer wait to feel like the person capable of change; you recognize that you are becoming that person through the steps you take.

It's important to understand that momentum is not linear. It accelerates, steadies, plateaus, dips, and returns. But once established, it becomes a resource you can return to. A pause does not erase the progress you've made; you pick up from where you've grown, not where you began. This is the gift of momentum: it preserves progress even through interruption.

Ultimately, momentum is about continuity. The willingness to return to movement after a pause, after a setback, or after an emotionally heavy day is what turns small steps into sustained transformation. Continuity turns effort into rhythm. Rhythm turns rhythm into capacity. And capacity is what prepares you for the next phase in the DO IT™ Method.

Momentum is proof that implementation is doing its job. It is the quiet engine that carries you through uncertainty, supports you when motivation is inconsistent, and bridges the gap between intention and transformation.

When Meaning Starts to Form

Everything you surfaced in DISCOVER—your current state, the impact you're navigating, the direction you're choosing, and why it matters—stops being conceptual during the implementation phase. Everything you claimed in OWN—your mindset, your stance, your choices—begins to take shape. Implementation is where you place your hands on the wheel of your life and learn what it means to guide your experience rather than be carried by it.

This phase is not glamorous. It demands patience, humility, and the willingness to keep moving even when your steps are small or your progress feels uneven. You'll meet resistance. You'll negotiate with old narratives. You'll have days when movement feels heavier than it should and others when you surprise yourself with strength you didn't know you had.

> But what people often overlook is that this is also the phase where your wins begin to show themselves and where acknowledging them becomes a genuine source of energy. You start to see the meaningful shifts: the message you finally sent, the boundary you upheld, the moment you chose rest instead of spiraling, the task you completed despite low motivation, or the decision you made from alignment rather than habit.

Recognizing these wins matters. Each one is evidence that something in you is shifting. Each one signals to your brain that the change is working. Each one reinforces your self-trust and strengthens your momentum. Celebration in this phase is not about hype—it is about acknowledgment. It is noticing what is different today from the version of you who felt stuck. It is giving weight to the progress that is easy to overlook because it does not announce itself loudly.

These moments of recognition also bring energy into a phase that can otherwise feel demanding. They remind you that movement is happening even when your emotions feel uncertain and help you see progress in places where doubt might cloud your perspective. They anchor your belief that the work you're doing is taking root. By intentionally recording these wins, small and significant, you create evidence of your progress and build momentum one step at a time, making the process tangible rather than theoretical.

There is something profoundly human about this stage. Through all the work, it dismantles the idea that transformation lives in your mind alone. Implementation teaches through experience and reveals that becoming does not require dramatic leaps; it requires consistent participation. And when your movement is paired with recognition, when your effort is allowed to register instead of being dismissed, you create the emotional and psychological lift that carries you naturally into the final phase of the DO IT Change Method™: Transform.

TRANSFORM is where the shifts you've practiced begin to integrate. It is where your identity catches up to your behavior, where meaning starts to form, and where the path behind you begins to make sense in a way it never could while you were walking it. Implementation has brought you here, to the threshold of who you are becoming.

In the next phase, you step into that identity fully.

CHAPTER 6

TRANSFORM

The Truth About Transformation (And Why This Chapter Almost Didn't Work)

When I first sat down to write this chapter, I found myself in a loop because I felt an unspoken pressure to deliver the type of transformation chapter the world is accustomed to. You know the version: the victorious climax, the cinematic breakthrough, the grand moment where everything crystallizes and you cross some invisible finish line with certainty, clarity, and triumphant energy.

The problem was simple: that version of transformation isn't true.

Not in real life. Not in meaningful change. Not in the work we've done throughout this method.

> No matter how beautifully we package the idea, transformation does not arrive wrapped like a Macy's Christmas gift or erupt like Fourth of July fireworks.

It doesn't knock on your door with fanfare or announce itself with a spotlight. And it certainly doesn't burst into your life the moment you think you've earned it.

So, I sat with that tension. I thought about the biggest shifts in my life—the planned, the unexpected, and the ones that tore through my world without warning. I thought about the seasons that shaped me, the transitions that stretched me, and the subtle recalibrations that remade me from the inside out. I wasn't searching for the most dramatic story; I was looking for the most *honest* one.

To my surprise, the story that rose to the top was not a life-altering crisis or an emotional breakthrough.

It was the day I decided, with complete conviction and zero preparation, to buy a manual car.

At first, that didn't feel worthy of a chapter this important.

But the more I sat with it, the more I realized that this story illustrates transformation more accurately than most of the "big" moments in my life ever could.

Because transformation rarely feels like transformation while it's happening.

It feels like practice.

Awkwardness.

Incremental progress.

Small wins you almost miss.

A subtle internal shift you only recognize in hindsight.

That's exactly what happened with that car.

And so, this chapter begins there because it mirrors the quiet way transformation actually takes shape within us.

The Manual Car

For as long as I can remember, I wanted to drive a manual. As a little girl, I loved cars, and I vividly remember watching my uncle shift gears, his hands moving with ease, attention fully engaged. I thought it was the coolest thing in the world.

My very first car was supposed to be one that was sleek, compact, and completely impractical for someone who had never touched a clutch. But the deal fell through, and practicality won. Life moved on, as it does. Bills. Commuting. Time constraints. Adulthood. The dream stayed tucked in the back of my mind, resurfacing now and then like a quiet whisper at a red light that said "One day."

Years passed, and that whisper stayed a whisper. The desire never faded, but responsibility has a way of convincing you that the things you want can wait. There were always more "reasonable" choices to make. A manual car never made it to the top of the list.

Until one random afternoon, when a commercial flashed across my TV announcing new-car promotions. Nothing special, just the usual sales event with big numbers and dramatic voice-overs. Still, I found myself thinking, *"Maybe I'll just go look."* I had never bought a brand-new car before, and curiosity nudged me out of the house.

I drove to the dealership with absolutely no intention of buying anything, let alone a manual. I was interested, but not invested. I browsed politely, test-drove a sensible automatic, made small talk with the salesperson... the usual routine. And then, out of nowhere, something in me shifted.

"Ask for a manual. This is your chance," that quiet voice spoke a little louder.

The thought came so quickly and clearly that I surprised myself. Before I could overthink it, I looked at the salesperson and said, "If you can find me a manual and if my payment is no more than five dollars above what I'm paying right now, I will buy it today."

He blinked. I blinked. And then he went to check.

A few minutes later, he came back with a look that said, *"You're not going to believe this."*

He found one.

A manual.

My dream transmission.

And the monthly payment? Three dollars more.

That was it. Decision made.

I traded in my car, signed the papers, and waited two days for it to arrive. When the call finally came, *"Your car is here,"* I felt electric. And also, wildly unprepared.

Because the truth was I had just bought a car I did not know how to drive.

So naturally, I called one of my best friends and asked the most chaotic favor possible.

"Hey! What are you doing? Want to come with me to pick up my new car and give me a crash course? It's a manual. I can't drive it."

She proceeded to call me a series of adjectives clearly questioning my sanity, but she came anyway.

We spent two hours in an empty parking lot, lurching, jerking, laughing, occasionally burning out the clutch because, let's be very clear, I never stalled, but I *definitely* jerked my way through those first attempts. She showed me how to feel the clutch engage, how to catch the gear, how to trust the timing. It was messy, loud, hilarious, and perfect.

Then came Monday morning.

If you've ever driven through DC rush-hour traffic, you know it is not for the faint of heart and certainly not ideal for someone who learned how to drive a manual twenty-four hours earlier. But there I was, merging onto the highway like someone who had momentarily lost touch with common sense but had absolutely found her courage.

Every morning that week, I drove to work shaking. Literally shaking. I wasn't afraid of crashing, but I was afraid of stalling in the middle of the highway with a thousand commuters behind me, honking me into oblivion. By the time I pulled into the office parking lot, I had to sit still for a minute just to convince my body that I was safe.

But by the second week, I noticed I wasn't shaking anymore. The gears were smoother, and my timing was steadier. My body was adapting.

After two months, I was a pro. I wasn't just managing—I was *mastering*. I even started intentionally finding hills just to test my skill. (Manual drivers know: a hill is where you separate the learners from the believers.)

The wildest part of the story is this: I didn't realize I transformed until months later.

I was telling someone the story, laughing about the parking lot lesson, the DC traffic, the ridiculous confidence it took to buy a car I couldn't drive, and somewhere between the laughter and the retelling, it hit me that I had changed.

And not at all in the dramatic, cinematic, transformational way we're conditioned to expect.

There was no lightning bolt or breakthrough moment.

No epiphany like a lit lightbulb.

Just practice.

Repetition.

Trying again.

Adjusting.

Getting better, almost without noticing.

One day I couldn't drive a manual. And then one day, months later, I realized I didn't remember what it felt like not to.

That is transformation.

Not the dramatic before-and-after.

Not the highlight reel.

Not the moment everything changes.

Transformation is the quiet shift that becomes obvious only in hindsight, the moment you recognize you're moving through the world with a different skill, a different mindset, a different identity than the one you started with.

That's why this story opens this chapter. Because it captures the truth every real transformation shares: You don't feel transformed while you're transforming.

You feel like someone who is learning.

Practicing.

Trying.

Messing up.

Trying again.

Becoming different through repetition.

The moment you realize you've changed is rarely the moment you actually changed. It's simply the moment you finally recognize it.

Transition Into Transformation

Learning to drive a manual car through awkward starts, shaky mornings, and quiet determination became one of the clearest mirrors of what real transformation looks like. Not the polished version we admire from afar. Not the glossy, over-promised version sold to us in motivational culture. But the lived version: ordinary in its daily demands yet extraordinary in its cumulative impact.

However, I didn't feel transformed while it was happening. I felt uncomfortable, stretched, focused, committed, and occasionally ridiculous. Every morning in that first week, I thought about calling out of work because the fear of driving was almost paralyzing. I went anyway. Transformation was the result of showing up for the experience again and again.

And that is why TRANSFORM is the final stage of the DO IT Change Method™.

It is the most human-focused stage, and you only recognize it once you're already living it.

What you're about to step into in this chapter is not a grand finale. It is a recalibration—a shift in how you move, how you think, how you respond, and ultimately, how you understand yourself.

> Transformation is not a moment at the top of a mountain; it is the moment you realize the climb has changed your capacity, endurance, resilience, and your ability to keep going even when the path steepens.

As those changes begin to take root, something else starts to happen—your inner work and your outer life begin moving in the same direction. That quiet alignment is the doorway into the next step of transformation: integration.

Integration: When the Internal and External Align

Integration is the quiet turning point in any change process. It's the moment when the work you have been doing internally begins to mirror the shifts occurring externally, creating a sense of coherence that may have felt out of reach at the beginning of your journey. Unlike the early stages of change, where your inner world and outer world often feel disconnected or even in conflict, integration brings a sense of alignment that is subtle, steady, and deeply grounding. During DISCOVER, you became aware of the reality you were standing in. During OWN, you clarified your stance and reclaimed your agency. During IMPLEMENT, you moved, adjusted, learned, and recalibrated. Integration is where these layers begin to fit together.

Integration is the phase where you stop oscillating between who you were and who you are becoming. The internal work stops feeling like practice and begins to feel like the foundation on which your daily life rests. Your thoughts, emotions, decisions, and behaviors begin to support one another rather than pull in different directions. You are moving toward a cohesive internal center.

This alignment shows up in different ways. You begin to navigate your life with a sense of internal consistency built on your ability to remain anchored when things fluctuate. Integration makes you less reactive, not because you have eliminated difficulty, but because your internal responses no longer escalate every time something shifts. You can experience discomfort without interpreting it as danger. You can face uncertainty without spiraling into catastrophic thinking, and you can make decisions without second-guessing every angle.

One of the clearest signs of integration is when your external choices begin to reflect your internal truths almost effortlessly. You make decisions that align with your values because those values are now clear to you. You remove yourself from environments that drain you because you no longer tolerate what is misaligned. You structure your life in ways that conserve your energy rather than deplete it. These choices are not driven by discipline alone—they are driven by congruence. You are now living in alignment.

Integration is reflected in how you relate to challenges. Instead of defaulting to old coping mechanisms—overthinking, withdrawing, overextending, numbing, or shrinking—you find yourself responding with greater presence. You may still feel discomfort or fear, but your actions are guided by the grounded version of you that has been quietly strengthening with every step you've taken. You no longer collapse into the past version of yourself when pressure rises; you reach toward the version you've been cultivating.

Externally, integration becomes visible in ways that others can sense even if they cannot name them. People may comment on your calmness, presence, boundaries, decisiveness, or your confidence. They may respond differently to you because your energy has shifted. You carry yourself with more intention, and the world responds accordingly.

In organizational change management, integration is the stage where a new system becomes "the way we do things now." The resistance diminishes. Teams stop referencing the past as the benchmark. The new rhythm stabilizes. The process becomes self-sustaining because it is no longer being imposed; it has been adopted. This is the hallmark of integration when the change no longer feels like something separate from daily life—it becomes part of it.

Your personal change follows this same pattern. Integration is not about completion; it is about internal coherence. It is not the absence of challenge, but the presence of alignment. It is not that everything becomes easy; it is that you are no longer working against yourself.

When your internal and external worlds begin moving in the same direction, you no longer waste energy trying to reconcile two conflicting realities. The emotional friction decreases. The mental noise quiets. The path ahead no longer feels like something you are chasing; it feels like something you are inhabiting. This is the essence of integration, the merging of your becoming with your being.

Transformation deepens and stabilizes here.

It becomes lived here.

The Subtle Recalibration of Identity

Identity is often spoken about as an established understanding of who you are, what you value, how you behave, and what you believe is possible for your life. But identity is not static. It stretches, contracts, evolves, and adapts in response to your lived experiences. When you navigate change intentionally, identity becomes one of the most profound areas of transformation because the parts of you that were dormant, underused, or overshadowed begin to take their rightful place.

The recalibration of identity does not begin with a bold proclamation of, "I am now this." It does not begin with a bold proclamation of "I am now this." Identity shifts in the same way dawn appears—so gradually that you often only recognize it once the light has already changed. You begin to feel a subtle distinction between the person who reacted automatically and the person who now responds with greater intention. You notice that you no longer see yourself solely through the lens of your past. Your sense of what is possible expands because *you* have expanded.

> Identity recalibrates when your actions, choices, mindset, and values begin to align with the version of yourself you have been steadily building throughout this change.

You no longer cling to the old stories about what you can or cannot do, who you have always been, or what you believe you deserve. These narratives do not disappear; simply lose their authority. They stop dictating your behavior and become part of your history rather than part of your decision-making.

This shift is subtle but powerful. You may notice that you speak about yourself differently. You acknowledge your strengths more clearly. You recognize your patterns without tying them to your worth. You give yourself credit for what you once dismissed. You stop performing for validation. You stop shrinking to maintain peace. You stop negotiating with versions of yourself that no longer reflect who you are. The recalibration is internal long before it becomes visible to others, but once it settles, the people around you begin to feel the difference as well.

Identity also recalibrates psychologically and neurologically. When you spend enough time practicing new behaviors, regulating your emotions, and taking action aligned with your values, your brain begins to update its internal model of who you are. This is biological. Neural pathways strengthen. Familiar responses weaken. Automatic behaviors shift. You begin to recognize yourself as capable, steady, resilient, and adaptive because your lived experiences now validate those qualities. The brain, always searching for patterns, begins to adopt this new pattern as your baseline.

With that internal shift comes something even more meaningful: the ability to tolerate being seen in your new identity. Many people underestimate how challenging this part can be. Becoming someone new is one thing; allowing others to experience that version of you is another. You may find that transformation requires renegotiating relationships, communicating boundaries with more clarity, or stepping into spaces that once intimidated you. You begin to allow yourself to be visible in ways that align with your growth. This visibility represents the external expression of the internal recalibration that has been quietly unfolding.

Identity recalibration is also marked by a shift in how you handle setbacks. The person you are becoming does not disappear when things go wrong. Instead of collapsing into the old narrative of defeat, you recover faster because your identity is no longer tangled in a fear-based interpretation of failure. You begin to see difficulty as information, not identity. You trust yourself to navigate discomfort because you have done it repeatedly throughout this process. You know how to return to your center because you built that center step by step.

Perhaps the most significant aspect of identity recalibration is the emergence of internal congruence. You begin to feel like yourself—not the version molded by fear, pleasing, survival, or habit, but the version shaped by intentionality, alignment, and truth. You experience a sense of quiet recognition, saying, *"This is who I am now. This is who I've been becoming all along."* It is not a loud realization, but a deeply grounding one. A moment where your internal world and external behaviors sit in harmony.

Transformation does not erase your past self; it integrates it. The parts of you that once operated from protection evolve into parts that operate from strength. The parts that once feared change begin to trust it. You do not abandon who you were, but you build upon it. Identity recalibration is the synthesis of every lesson, choice, mistake, insight, and step that has carried you to this point.

This recalibration is not about becoming a perfected version of yourself. It is about becoming a more aligned one. A more honest one. A more expanded one. A self that can hold contradiction, navigate uncertainty, trust its wisdom, and move through the world with a steadiness that comes from evidence, not wishful thinking.

Identity doesn't shift because you declare it. It shifts because you live it. And in the final movements of Transform, that lived identity becomes the new baseline from which your life begins to unfold.

And because identity evolves quietly through lived experience, it becomes easier to see transformation in retrospect than in the moment. The clearest indicators of transformation are found in the way a person responds differently to a familiar challenge, initiates a new chapter with confidence, or navigates loss with a depth of resilience they did not know they possessed.

This is why the examples that follow matter. They show identity recalibration *in motion*—across the three major categories of change: anticipated, unexpected, and life-altering.

Each example illustrates not only how DO IT™ guides the process, but how a person's sense of self shifts as they move through it. They are stories of subtle, grounded internal evolution—the kind that transforms how a person lives, decides, relates, and moves through the world long after the change itself has passed.

Real Example 1 — Anticipated Change: The Dream He Finally Stopped Delaying

For nearly a decade, Maya carried a quiet dream to launch a small creative studio that helped individuals and teams develop concepts, refine ideas, and bring creative projects to life. It lived only in the notes app on her phone and in late-night conversations with friends. She always planned to begin "soon," but soon stretched into years. She convinced herself she was waiting for stability, confidence, or the "right season," but the truth was that she feared being seen in the messy beginning.

DISCOVER was the moment she admitted that fear out loud with honesty. She realized she had been protecting herself from vulnerability more than she was protecting her time. Every excuse had become a shield against the fear of starting small.

In OWN, she made a shift that changed everything: her dream was no longer optional. It was part of who she was becoming. She decided to treat it as a responsibility rather than a luxury because she no longer wanted to live a life where her aspirations stayed theoretical.

Implementation was built on imperfect action. It looked like drafting content after work when she was tired, watching tutorials in between errands, redesigning her logo six times, and letting one friend in on the plan so accountability could replace secrecy. None of it was glamorous. None of it made her feel "ready." But each small effort placed a brick in the identity she was building.

And then, transformation arrived. She noticed it the first time she introduced herself as "working on a creative studio" without apologizing or laughing it off. She noticed it when someone asked what she did, and instead of shrinking, she answered with calm certainty. She noticed it the morning she revised her website and caught herself thinking like a business owner instead of a hobbyist.

But the clearest moment came the day she pressed "post."

She had expected shaking hands or a rush of panic, but instead she felt a grounded stillness. Her breath was steady. Her shoulders relaxed. Her mind wasn't scanning for judgment; it was simply present.

When the first message came in, a stranger saying, "I've been waiting for someone to offer this," she whispered to herself, "I'm really doing this," with recognition.

Maya's transformation wasn't the act of posting; it was the quiet internal restructuring that allowed her to do it without fear defining her.

She didn't just launch a business. She stepped into the identity of someone who builds the life she wants.

Real Example 2 — Unexpected Change: Learning to Care Without Disappearing

Patrice had never imagined she would become her husband's primary caregiver before fifty. His sudden diagnosis rearranged her world in an instant. Overnight, she became the center of his support system, managing appointments, medications, emotions, and logistics while trying desperately not to dissolve under the weight of it all.

DISCOVER came in a difficult but liberating confession. She was exhausted, grieving the life she used to have, and quietly terrified she would disappear inside this role. She admitted she needed help—something she had spent years believing she should never ask for.

In OWN, she shifted her stance from silent martyrdom to intentional participation. She questioned the belief that sacrificing herself was the only way to prove love. She allowed herself to acknowledge that her needs were not obstacles to his healing, and they were essential to it.

Implementation was made of small recalibrations.

She asked her sister to take one evening each week.

She joined a caregiver support group.

She started taking two hours on Saturday mornings just to breathe, walk, and return to herself.

Transformation didn't arrive when life got easier; it arrived when *she* became steadier.

She recognized it on a quiet Saturday morning when her husband asked, "Could you run to the pharmacy now? I forgot to mention I need a refill."

For months, she had rearranged her entire schedule around these last-minute needs, without question.

But this time, something in her paused.

"I can go this afternoon, but not right this minute."

And the miracle wasn't in the words; it was in her body because her voice didn't tremble, her throat didn't tighten, and guilt didn't rise like a wave.

She took two hours. She returned settled, present, and able to care from fullness instead of depletion.

Her transformation continued revealing itself:

She stopped apologizing for resting.

She stopped interpreting help as weakness.

She began showing up from steadiness.

She started planning small things for her future, even while caregiving continued.

Patrice's transformation wasn't an escape from responsibility. It was an integration of herself *within* it.

She learned the truth she once feared: She could care deeply for her husband without disappearing inside his diagnosis.

Real Example 3 — Life-Altering Change: Reclaiming Presence After the Life He Knew Ended

Noah's life changed in a single moment.

A sudden and violent car accident left him with permanent physical limitations and a recovery timeline that erased every assumption he had about his future. Before the accident, he had defined himself through movement, independence, and reliability. After the accident, even simple tasks required assistance, patience, and constant recalibration.

In the weeks that followed, Noah focused on surgeries, appointments, physical therapy, and insurance forms. He complied and endured, but internally, he was unraveling. The loss wasn't only physical, it was psychological. The man he had been no longer fit the life he was now living.

DISCOVER arrived quietly, months after the accident, during an ordinary moment that shouldn't have mattered. He reached for something he used to do without thinking and realized he couldn't. Not yet. Maybe not ever.

The frustration that surfaced surprised him with its intensity. What followed wasn't just anger. It was grief. Grief for his body, his independence, and for the version of himself he kept trying to return to.

For the first time, Noah stopped telling himself he was "fine."

He admitted that he wasn't just recovering from an injury. He was grieving a life that no longer existed.

In OWN, Noah shifted his stance.

He couldn't undo the accident.

He couldn't rush his body back to what it had been.

But he could choose how he related to this new reality.

He acknowledged a truth that felt both grounding and terrifying: If he kept measuring himself against who he used to be, he would stay trapped in loss. If he wanted stability, he had to meet himself where he was.

That decision didn't fix anything overnight, but it gave him agency. He stopped fighting reality and began working with it.

IMPLEMENT unfolded slowly and deliberately.

He worked with his physical therapist to redefine progress, focusing on function rather than comparison. He asked for help instead of pushing through pain to prove something to himself, and he established routines that supported his energy rather than draining it. Journaling became useful to track what was improving, even when it felt insignificant. He practiced grounding techniques when frustration spiked, orienting himself back to what his body *could* do instead of what it couldn't.

Some days were discouraging, and some days he was proud of his progress. There were days when he felt patient, and some days he had no patience for the process. But he kept showing up, not to "get back to normal," but to stay present with the life he was actually living.

TRANSFORM revealed itself gradually.

Noah noticed he no longer introduced himself by what he had lost.

He began recognizing strength in adaptability rather than endurance.

He stopped waiting for his old life to return and started building a new one, intentionally, realistically, and with compassion.

The transformation was about acceptance and integration.

He became someone who trusted himself to navigate limitations without collapsing into them.

Someone who understood that identity could evolve without disappearing.

Someone grounded in what remained—and what was still possible.

Noah didn't return to the life he had before the accident. Instead, he built a life that fit who he had become, one rooted in presence, agency, and the quiet confidence that he could meet whatever came next.

The New Baseline: Living From Your Transformed Self

The new baseline is the first measurable shift in how you move through your life after doing the work of change. Not a dramatic breakthrough or a sudden surge of inspiration, but a different internal posture that begins to shape your everyday decisions, reactions, and interpretations.

Before transformation, your baseline is shaped by automatic reactions built from survival, habit, and history. But as the work of DISCOVER, OWN, and IMPLEMENT recalibrates your system, those reflexes begin to lose their authority. You show up to situations with a steadier center and a clearer sense of how you want to respond.

This new baseline asks you to become consistent. It means your relationship with yourself is no longer dictated by fear or avoidance, but by alignment. You still experience frustration, doubt, exhaustion, or overwhelm, but you recover faster. You find your footing sooner. You stay connected to your values even when the moment is challenging.

The markers of this baseline are specific:

Your internal dialogue evolves.

The voice that once spiraled now evaluates. The voice that once criticized now questions. The voice that once assumed catastrophe now searches for context.

Your emotional processing strengthens.

You feel the wave of anger, sadness, fear, and uncertainty, but you no longer lose access to the part of you capable of making grounded decisions.

Your behaviors shift toward alignment.

You speak more directly. You protect your energy without apology. You set boundaries without the emotional hangover. You follow through without bargaining yourself out of your goals.

Your sense of possibility expands.

You consider opportunities from desire instead of fear. You move toward what feels right rather than what feels safe. You let yourself imagine futures that once felt out of reach.

This new baseline is the first structural outcome of transformation. It changes how you move through conflict, pursue goals, interpret stress, and inhabit your life. You haven't become a new person, but you've become a more coherent version of yourself.

From here, transformation deepens into something even more meaningful, a shift in how you relate to your past, your identity, and the evidence of who you now are.

Embodiment: When Your Past Stops Running the Show

Embodiment is the phase where transformation becomes structural. It's the point where your past no longer dictates how you interpret yourself, your limits, or your possibilities. You aren't rewriting your history; you're reorganizing your relationship with it.

Before embodiment, your past carries the weight of old patterns that feel familiar, old reflexes that feel automatic, old interpretations that feel true simply because they're practiced. As your new baseline strengthens, something more profound begins to occur as you gain the capacity to see your past without living from it.

> In embodiment, the past stops functioning as a warning system and becomes useful information. You understand *why* you protected yourself the way you did, *why* certain patterns developed, and *why* certain seasons stretched you thin. But you no longer confuse those patterns with your identity.

A shift takes place: You stop organizing your present through the lens of what hurt you.

You stop assuming that past outcomes predict your future abilities.

You stop shrinking in anticipation of an old story repeating itself.

As that shift changes, a different kind of confidence begins to take shape, earned confidence grounded in lived evidence.

Evidence that you can remain steady in moments you once avoided.

Evidence that you can move through discomfort without abandoning yourself.

Evidence that you can choose the aligned response even when the easy one calls your name.

Evidence that you can trust your judgment because you have proven to yourself that your decisions can hold.

This is why embodiment feels different from the new baseline.

The baseline is about consistency.

Embodiment is about identity.

In this phase, the progress has become part of how you operate. The version of you that once felt aspiration becomes the version of you that feels natural. You're not forcing new behaviors; those behaviors reflect who you now understand yourself to be. This is the heart of TRANSFORM within the DO IT Change Method™.

A fully integrated self. A self who can meet the next change, gentle or jarring, expected or disruptive, with coherence, stability, and a grounded sense of who they are.

Embodiment is the foundation that makes every future evolution possible.

The Quiet Arrival of Who You've Become

The DO IT Change Method™ was never intended to turn you into someone else or to replace the core of who you are. Its purpose has always been to return you to yourself—to the clearer, steadier, more grounded version of you that emerges when you stop navigating change from a place of fear and begin navigating it with intention. By the time you reach the TRANSFORM stage, the heaviest work is already behind you. You have confronted your reality with honesty, without minimizing what needed to be faced or inflating what you feared. You have taken responsibility for your role in the journey—neither blaming yourself for what you could not control nor denying the influence you do have. You have acted with courage even when certainty was unavailable, allowing movement to teach you what stillness could not. And you have remained open to the lessons the process offered, even when those lessons stretched you emotionally, mentally, and sometimes physically. Transformation is simply the moment when all of these efforts begin to take shape inside you in a coherent, integrated way.

This point in your evolution is evidence that you can continue growing, continue choosing intentionally, and continue shaping your life in ways that honor you. Your identity is no longer defined by the protective patterns that once limited you; it is shaped by the proof you've created through lived experience that you can respond with intention, shift with honesty, and trust the sound of your voice. These qualities are part of you.

From here, your life does not suddenly become easier or more predictable. What changes is your ability to navigate it. You carry a different level of emotional capacity, a different relationship with uncertainty, and a different understanding of who you are in the presence of change. The difficulties you encounter will still require strength, discernment, and patience, but you will approach them from a centered place rather than a reactive one. You have built an internal foundation that steadies you, even when the world outside of you feels uncertain.

You will experience more change. You will encounter moments that challenge you. You will meet versions of yourself you haven't yet grown into. But unlike before, you now possess a framework that can hold you, guide you, and remind you of your agency when life becomes complex. The DO IT Change Method™ is not a one-time process; it is a method you can return to whenever you feel yourself drifting, whenever a transition demands more of you, or whenever a new season invites you into becoming someone fuller and more aligned.

In the next chapter, we walk directly toward those hurdles to understand how to move through them without losing the composure, agency, and strength you have built so intentionally.

Chapter 7

Overcoming the Hurdles

The Phase Most People Mistake for Failure

This chapter will show you that the hurdles you face after doing the work are not evidence that you're going backward, but they are evidence that the change is taking root.

Most people misinterpret this part of the journey. They assume that once they've "done the work," gained insight, or taken action, the difficulty should end. They expect the path to open up, smooth out, and stay steady. So, when challenges reappear, motivation dips, old emotions resurface, or unexpected waves of resistance hit, they panic and question their progress. They question themselves.

> It's important to remember that the challenges are not signs of regression; they are signs that your system is adjusting to your new direction.

When you shift deeply—emotionally, mentally, behaviorally, or in identity—your system has to reorganize itself around who you are becoming. That reorganization creates friction. It is the same kind of friction an athlete feels when strengthening a new muscle group, the same friction a leader experiences when a team adjusts to a new vision, the same friction a person encounters when breaking long-held patterns. It's uncomfortable because it's unfamiliar.

In fact, the presence of these hurdles often signals that you are no longer operating on autopilot.

You are awake, not going through the motions.

You notice what once went unnoticed.

You respond in ways your old identity never could have.

This is progress, but if you don't understand this, it's easy to assume you're slipping backward. You're not. You're stabilizing, strengthening, and learning how to live from the self you've been building. This stage is less about eliminating hurdles and more about learning to interpret them correctly, so you don't mistake normal human complexity for personal failure.

This chapter won't promise you a perfect path. It will give you something better, a grounded understanding of what's normal, what's not, and how to keep moving when the journey gets messy.

Why We Expect Cinematic-Style Change

Every meaningful change carries an emotional landscape marked by rises, dips, plateaus, and unexpected turns. And yet, most people expect the exact opposite. They imagine that once they've committed, their motivation should rise on a steady upward climb. That once they take the first step, everything else should fall into place. That doing the "right" work should immediately feel good, or at least consistent.

But that belief did not come out of thin air. We've been conditioned—culturally, socially, and psychologically—to expect transformation to feel cinematic and unmistakable, as if there should be a clear turning point you can identify the moment it happens.

Movies, books, speeches, and success stories all showcase this breakthrough moment of clarity, the triumphant pivot, the clean before-and-after. We highlight the dramatic scene, not the months of private struggle, stalled attempts, internal negotiation, and emotional chaos that actually produced the shift.

Culturally, we celebrate outcomes far more loudly than we celebrate the process. We applaud the promotion, not the years of insecurity. We admire the healed version of someone, not the nights they doubted whether healing was possible. We broadcast the moment someone "arrived," not the recalibrations that got them there. We've been taught to chase the moment everything supposedly "clicks."

Culture feeds us curated highlight reels.

Movies hand us dramatic breakthroughs tied up in perfect scenes.

Social media presents the filtered, edited "after," without any trace of the work underneath.

But the part between the beginning and the breakthrough, where the transformation *actually happens,* is almost always edited out.

You know how films show a quick montage where the character goes from struggling to thriving? Upbeat music, quick flashes of effort, and suddenly everything has changed. Take *The Pursuit of Happyness*. In the final scene, Chris Gardner stands in the street with tears in his eyes, finally offered the job that would change his life. It feels like a single moment transformed him. The movie gives us the payoff, but it leaves out the part where the transformation actually settles:

- the first weeks in that new job when he felt like a fraud
- the mornings he questioned whether he could keep up
- the days he worried his luck would run out
- the pressure of suddenly being the "success story" without feeling successful
- the adjustment to a new routine, new expectations, new scrutiny
- the fear of losing everything he had just gained

- the silent, private recalibration after the big moment everyone remembers

- the nights he wondered if he'd made the right long-term choice

- the new apartment he could barely afford and the longer commute that drained him

- the tension between being grateful and being overwhelmed

None of that survives the editing room. It isn't cinematic or marketable. It's the part that's too ordinary to glamorize, and that's the problem. We're conditioned to believe that transformation ends at the breakthrough, but the breakthrough is just the doorway. The actual transformation happens in the unglamorous steps that come after, in the repetition, the practice, the doubt, and the incremental shifts that don't look like progress but are.

Because the nervous system naturally prefers predictability, we want change to make emotional sense, and our minds tell us progress has to *feel* like progress. We want discomfort to be brief, so we create stories that make growth feel linear, even though real change rarely operates that way.

So when your journey doesn't feel like a rising soundtrack or a dramatic turning point, nothing is wrong. You're not behind or doing it incorrectly. You're simply in the part where transformation becomes real.

The Emotional Hills and Valleys of Change

The emotional experience of change has been studied for decades, and every credible framework—from the Kübler-Ross Change Curve to Fisher's Personal Transition Curve to the J-Curve in organizational transformation—tells us the same truth: change brings emotional highs, lows, dips, spikes, and everything in between.

Even when the change is aligned or deeply desired, emotional consistency is rare. Some days you feel energized and other days you question everything. Sometimes you feel clear and grounded, and other times you feel pulled back toward old habits or old fears. These fluctuations don't signal regression; they simply reflect the recalibration happening under the surface.

> When you begin doing something unfamiliar, your brain becomes more alert. It is assessing risk, scanning for threats, and trying to determine whether this new direction is safe. This can make you feel more sensitive, tired, reactive, or emotionally unpredictable, but this is just your biology adjusting, as it is designed to.

The protective parts of you, the ones shaped by past experiences, survival strategies, or emotional conditioning, will rise when they sense change. They are not acting against you; they are simply trying to keep you safe using outdated information.

One of the most overlooked realities of change is that even positive change carries a form of grief. Any time you step into something new, you are also leaving something familiar behind—a routine you once depended on, a role you once inhabited, or a version of yourself you no longer need. That letting go has an emotional cost.

> Grief and growth often walk side by side. You can expand and still feel the ache of what you're releasing. You can move forward and still feel the pull of what once grounded you. This is evidence that the change is real.

Why Change Isn't Linear

Change affects your identity, your nervous system, your routines, your relationships, your beliefs, your sense of safety, your perceived competence, and your internalized narratives about who you are. When so many layers of your life are shifting at the same time, the emotional outcomes cannot—and will not—move in a tidy, linear progression. Real change is multidimensional, and multidimensional processes never produce one-dimensional pathways.

Even when you want to move forward, your brain may briefly pull you backward because the old pathways are still firing alongside the new ones. Neuroplasticity and synaptic pruning are two processes in the brain that explain *why* change feels messy, nonlinear, and sometimes contradictory.

Neuroplasticity is your brain's ability to form new pathways, such as new habits, new emotional responses, new interpretations, new behaviors. Every time you practice a new pattern (a boundary, a habit, a coping skill, a perspective), your brain strengthens a fresh neural route.

Synaptic pruning is the flip side. It's the brain's way of clearing out old connections you no longer use. The pathways tied to your old habits, reactions, patterns, and identities will fade slowly over time as your brain stops reinforcing them.

This combination is why change feels inconsistent. You're strengthening something new while simultaneously weakening something old, and both processes take time. That's why some days you respond with your new tools, and other days an old reflex slips through. Instead of viewing it as a failure, remember that your brain is literally rewiring itself and it doesn't happen overnight.

Organizational change models reinforce this reality. The Bridges Transition Model highlights the "neutral zone," a phase of ambiguity and instability that people must pass through before embracing the new beginning. Lewin's Unfreeze-Change-Refreeze model acknowledges that the "unfreezing" phase alone can create emotional chaos before any positive momentum emerges. These frameworks were built to describe group behavior, yet their logic translates seamlessly to individual lives: disruption precedes integration.

Nonlinearity is also tied to your environment. Your responsibilities, relationships, finances, time constraints, health, emotional bandwidth, and support systems all influence your pace. Life does not pause simply because you are changing. External pressures may cause you to accelerate one moment and slow down the next. The danger is in misinterpreting the nature of change. When you understand that progress contracts before it expands, that consistency is built through cycles rather than straight lines, and that emotional variability is part of the recalibration process, you stop taking the fluctuations personally. You begin to see the dips for what they are: pauses, refinements, and integration.

This shift in understanding changes everything. It frees you from the unrealistic expectation that healing or reinvention should follow a predictable timeline. It gives you space to be human in the process rather than demanding that you perform stability you don't yet possess. And it allows you to maintain momentum even when the emotional rhythm of change feels unpredictable. When you stop expecting linearity, you stop abandoning yourself mid-journey.

What You're Experiencing Is More Common Than You Think

One of the most powerful gifts you can give yourself during change is an accurate understanding of what "normal" looks and feels like. It is normal:

To feel motivated one day and uncertain the next. This inconsistency reflects the shifting interplay between your emotions, your nervous system, and the cognitive load of adapting to something unfamiliar. Change requires energy. Some days you have more to give, other days less.

To feel discomfort, even when the change is positive. People often assume that desirable change should feel energizing, empowering, or exciting at every step. Discomfort is not a signal that the change is misaligned. In fact, feeling uncomfortable is one of the clearest indicators that you've stepped out of your old framework and into something new.

To revisit old feelings or patterns as you move forward. Progress does not permanently eliminate doubt, fear, or old habits. They may resurface in moments of stress or uncertainty, because the brain often reactivates familiar patterns when it feels overwhelmed. This is part of the recalibration process. What matters is how you respond to them now.

For your confidence to fluctuate. Confidence is not a constant state; it is a dynamic one. When you engage with unfamiliar territory, your internal sense of competence naturally shifts. Some actions reinforce your confidence, and others stretch you in ways that temporarily make you question yourself. This oscillation is a sign of expansion.

To feel grief, even if the change is something you chose. Many people underestimate the emotional complexity of leaving behind what was familiar. You may grieve the predictability of your old routine, the identity you once carried, the role you once held, or the comfort of knowing who you were in a previous season. This grief means you are honoring what once supported you.

To feel tired. Change is metabolically expensive as your brain and body are actively working. Your brain is building new neural pathways, your body is adjusting to new patterns, and your emotional system is processing layers of meaning, memory, and expectation. Fatigue indicates that your system is actively working. Just as a muscle strengthens through resistance and rest, your capacity builds through effort and recovery.

To question yourself. Self-doubt does not mean the change is wrong. It means the change matters. Any significant transition asks you to step into a version of yourself you haven't fully lived yet. Questioning is part of the mental negotiation between who you were and who you are becoming. Doubt only becomes a barrier when you interpret it as a stop sign rather than a signal to proceed thoughtfully.

For change to take longer than expected. Timelines you envisioned may stretch in reality because life is layered, responsibilities shift, emotions fluctuate, and change interacts with the rest of your human experience. There is no meaningful transformation that adheres perfectly to a calendar. Progress unfolds at the intersection of readiness, capacity, support, and circumstance.

To experience relational tension. When you begin to shift, the people around you may need time to adjust. Some will support your growth immediately; others may struggle with the unfamiliar version of you who now communicates more clearly, holds firmer boundaries, or acts with greater agency. Their discomfort is part of the broader system recalibrating to your transformation.

This tension is one of the most underestimated challenges of change. When familiar dynamics are disrupted, subtle pressures can emerge such as teasing, doubt, guilt, withdrawal, or unspoken expectations to "go back to normal." These reactions can make old habits feel safer than forward movement. They can tempt you to soften your boundaries, quiet your voice, or return to patterns that no longer serve you.

Recognizing relational tension as part of the process helps you stay oriented. It allows you to distinguish between discomfort that signals growth and discomfort that signals misalignment. When you expect this resistance, you are less likely to interpret it as failure and more likely to remain steady long enough for the people around you to adjust.

To return to earlier phases of DO IT™, DISCOVER, OWN, IMPLEMENT, and TRANSFORM are practices. When the emotional terrain becomes confusing, you may need to revisit Discovery. When a new fear emerges, you may need to re-engage Ownership. When momentum stalls, you may need to refine your steps in Implementation. The method is designed to move with you.

When you understand what is normal, you no longer mislabel the natural rhythms of change as signs of inadequacy. You stop pathologizing the very experiences that signify your growth and begin to offer yourself the compassion, patience, and grounding that change requires. And most importantly, you stop giving unnecessary power to the moments that feel difficult, because you understand that difficulty is woven into every meaningful transition.

Recognizing what is normal does not eliminate the challenges, but it strips them of their ability to derail you. It anchors you in the truth that you are not struggling because you are incapable; you are experiencing exactly what every human experiences when they grow. And from that grounded understanding, you're ready for the next part of the journey: what to do when you feel like you've fallen off track.

Chapter 8

You Got This

The Strength You Built Without Realizing It

"You got this" is not a slogan in this book. It is not cheer-leading, optimism, or a borrowed affirmation meant to temporarily inflate your courage. It is an acknowledgment of the truth you have proven to yourself across every chapter that came before this. By the time you reach this point in the DO IT Change Method™, you have already demonstrated a level of resilience, intentionality, and emotional maturity that most people never slow down long enough to recognize. I wrote this chapter to help you finally see that strength for yourself.

People often underestimate their capacity because they only measure it by how well they hold themselves together during the hardest moments. But your strength is not defined by how perfectly you navigated change. It is defined by the fact that you showed up for the journey at all. It is reflected in the moments you named truths that were uncomfortable and in the decisions you made when certainty was unavailable. It is evidenced by the small steps you took when momentum felt fragile, and in the internal shifts you committed to even when you doubted yourself. Strength is rarely loud in the moment, and it reveals itself in retrospect, when you realize how many times you could have walked away from your growth and didn't.

> "You got this" recognizes that you are no longer participating in change from instinct or fear. You are navigating it with structure, intention, and a growing sense of personal authority.

Whether the change you are facing is anticipated, unexpected, or life-altering, you are now equipped with a framework that grounds you in reality, anchors your mindset, clarifies your choices, guides your actions, and integrates your transformation. This is no small accomplishment. It is a shift in how you move through your life.

What makes this moment powerful is that the confidence you feel now is earned. It comes from evidence, not wishful thinking. It comes from the inner work you have already done, the honest reflection you engaged in, the emotional courage you practiced, and the steps you took even when you didn't feel ready. You have participated fully in your change, and participation is where self-trust grows. Even when you didn't move perfectly, you moved intentionally. And that matters far more.

This chapter is your reminder of who you have become while doing this work. The confidence you feel now is a reflection of the internal stability you have been building piece by piece, and that stability is what makes you capable of facing whatever comes next.

Your Capability Runs Deeper Than Your Doubt

Even if you don't always believe it, you are far more capable than you realize. You are capable of changing careers, rebuilding after betrayal, losing fifty pounds, leaving an unhealthy relationship, moving to a new city, learning new skills at any age, returning to school, starting a business, healing old patterns, and creating a life you've never seen modeled. You can do all of these things for one reason: you are capable.

Capability is your ability to stretch, to learn, to adapt, to try again, to rebuild, to tolerate discomfort, to figure things out as you go, and to keep yourself moving even when you feel overwhelmed. Capability is already in you. It doesn't need to be installed; it needs to be activated.

The real question is not *Can you?* It is "*Will you?*" Will you take the step even when you're unsure? Will you speak up even when your voice shakes? Will you hold the boundary even when someone pushes back? Will you follow through even when motivation dips? Will you keep going even when the outcome is not guaranteed? This is where courage enters.

Courage is what turns capability into action. It is not boldness, fearlessness, or confidence. Courage is the willingness to move *with* fear, to act in the presence of uncertainty, hesitation, doubt, or emotional resistance. It is the internal "yes" that rises before you feel ready. It is the decision to choose alignment over comfort. It is the part of you that says, "I may be scared, but I'm still going."

Capability says you can.

Courage determines whether you will.

And when capability and courage finally meet, that is where meaningful, sustainable transformation takes place.

You've Been Doing This Your Entire Life

Your ability to hold discomfort, make intentional choices, take imperfect action, and integrate what you've learned is not something new. It's something you've been doing since the very beginning of your life. From infancy to adulthood, you have adapted to every new demand placed in front of you. Your body evolved, your thinking evolved, your identity evolved, and your world evolved, and you have kept pace with all of it, often without noticing how much strength and flexibility that required.

You learned to walk long before you trusted your balance. You learned to speak before you fully understood the power or meaning of your voice. You learned to navigate people long before you grasped the complexity of relationships. Every chapter of your life has been shaped by this same pattern: incremental growth, small attempts that eventually became confidence, and ongoing recalibration that eventually became identity. Adaptation has always been the foundation.

That pattern didn't disappear when you became an adult; it simply became less visible. Capability began to blend into the background because it was expected. Courage became quieter because life grew louder. Adaptability stopped being celebrated because people assumed you already knew how to manage yourself. But none of it vanished. It's been operating beneath the surface, waiting for you to reconnect with it.

The DO IT Change Method™ didn't create qualities you lacked. It helps you see the ones you've carried all along. It helps you name the skills that were already there, and use them with intention rather than instinct. It reminds you that you have always known how to evolve. You are someone who has moved through shifting seasons, unexpected events, emotional valleys, identity shifts, and new beginnings long before you ever saw the DO IT framework on a page. You have met change, navigated it, learned from it, and rebuilt yourself through it, often without giving yourself much credit.

This isn't motivational language. It's an honest reflection of your history, your biology, and the evidence of your lived experience. You are now far more capable than you believed at the beginning of this journey, and far more courageous than your hardest moments tried to convince you. These two truths will carry you into every life chapter ahead because you are now more aligned with who you truly are and more aware of the strength you've always had.

The Control You Actually Have

We talked about control earlier in this book—how fear distorts it, how uncertainty narrows it, and how quickly it can get tangled with perfectionism or helplessness. But control is so central to how humans experience change, so tied to agency, stability, and emotional regulation, that it deserves to be revisited here with a more refined lens.

Your relationship with control shapes your relationship with change. It influences how you interpret challenges, how quickly you recover, how confidently you take your next step, and how willing you are to participate in your evolution. The way you understand control will either steady you or destabilize you in every transition.

This is why we return to it now, so you recognize the kind of control that strengthens you, not the kind you were conditioned to chase. By this point in the DO IT Change Method™, you've likely discovered that the control you once thought you lacked wasn't missing. You were simply trying to access it in the wrong places.

Most people approach control in extremes: either trying to manage everything or collapsing into the belief that they control nothing. Real control is neither. Real control lives in the middle. It is the influence you have over your posture, your participation, your interpretation, and your next step. It is actionable.

This matters now more than ever, because every chapter before this one—DISCOVER, OWN, IMPLEMENT, TRANSFORM, and the recalibrations of Chapter 7—has been quietly reinforcing the same truth that you always have some form of control, even when the landscape feels unpredictable. Not total control, but meaningful control that stabilizes you internally even when life is shifting externally.

The problem is that most people try to control the wrong things such as the outcome, the timeline, other people's reactions, the speed of progress, or the entire unfolding of the change itself. Those forms of control rarely hold, and when they fall apart, people assume *they* failed. But what actually failed was the strategy.

Trying to manage what lies outside your influence breeds anxiety, exhaustion, and a distorted sense of capability. When you redirect your energy toward what *is* within your influence, your internal conditions—your interpretation, emotional regulation, boundaries, communication, environment, and willingness to engage—you reclaim the parts of the journey that always belonged to you.

External conditions are the aspects of your environment you can't fully control but can meaningfully shape such as your routines, the systems you create, the support you seek, the space you work or live in, the boundaries you communicate, and the resources you engage. You may not control every external factor, but you absolutely influence the environment you move through, and that influence matters more than people realize.

When you anchor yourself in these internal and external conditions, your nervous system settles. Your clarity returns. Your self-trust strengthens. You shift from trying to survive the change to actively guiding it. And with each intentional decision, your sense of control grows because you are operating from a steadier center.

> Most people wait to *feel* in control before they act, but it's not a feeling. Control is a practice created *through* action. Every moment you regulate your emotions, choose your posture, set a boundary, or take a step, you reclaim influence over your experience. These micro-acts compound and form a new baseline. They become evidence that you can trust yourself even when the outcome is unknown.

You don't need total control to move forward with confidence.

You just need enough control to guide your next intentional step.

You've had it throughout this entire journey.

Now you see it more clearly, and awareness turns control from something you hoped for into something you can rely on.

The Posture You Carry Forward

By the time you reach this stage in the DO IT Change Method™, the question is not *whether* you can navigate change. The question becomes how you will carry yourself as you continue doing it. The posture you hold—internally and externally—shapes everything that comes next. It determines whether you meet future change with steadiness or fear, with intentionality or reactivity, with self-trust or self-doubt.

This posture reflects the way you orient yourself toward what's ahead. It is the way you approach uncertainty, the way you interpret discomfort, the way you return to yourself when life becomes complicated. Your posture is the way you stand within your identity.

The posture you carry forward is built from the work you've already done. You learned in DISCOVER that telling the truth gives you solid ground to stand on, even when the truth is uncomfortable. That becomes part of your posture. You learned in OWN that you influence your internal experience even when you don't control the external conditions. That becomes part of your posture. You learned in IMPLEMENT that progress is created through movement, not perfection. That becomes part of your posture. You learned in TRANSFORM that identity shifts begin internally long before the world notices. That too becomes part of your posture.

> Together, these experiences create a way of navigating your life that is more discerning than before. You begin noticing the difference between reacting and responding, between fear speaking and intuition guiding, between urgency pulling you forward and alignment moving you forward.

This discernment is the recognition that you do not have to mirror everything you feel. You can feel uncertainty without becoming destabilized by it. You can experience doubt without abandoning your direction. You can be stretched without losing your grounding.

Carrying this posture forward also changes the way you relate to challenges. Instead of interpreting obstacles as threats, you begin to see them as something to navigate rather than something to fear. You become less preoccupied with predicting every outcome and more focused on meeting each moment with intention. Your capacity to regulate your emotions expands. Your ability to hear your internal voice strengthens. You develop a steadiness that isn't rigid, but firm enough to hold you and flexible enough to adapt.

Most importantly, your posture becomes an active choice rather than a passive default. You are no longer shaped solely by your circumstances; you participate in shaping your experience of them. This is the quiet advantage of transformation: as your internal structure becomes more coherent, your external steps become more aligned. Your decisions feel more grounded, and your relationship with yourself is steady.

This posture will not eliminate uncertainty, but it will change your proximity to it. You will still encounter moments that challenge your patience, resilience, or emotional bandwidth. But these moments will meet a different version of you—one who understands that steadiness is something you cultivate, not wait for. One who knows that emotional fluctuation is not evidence of failure; it is evidence of being alive. One who remembers that movement counts, even when the pace is uneven.

This is the posture you carry forward, one that is grounded, intentional, and rooted in the evidence of who you have become in a way that honors your capacity, protects your energy, and keeps you tethered to your truth as you step into whatever comes next.

You Are Ready for Your Life

Weather-Proofing for Change

Let's end this chapter with something simple: the weather.

Let me admit this upfront: "extreme cold" is a subjective term. For some people, extreme cold means temperatures so frigid they freeze eyelashes. For me, anything below fifty degrees Fahrenheit has me reevaluating every decision that brought me outside in the first place. Regardless of what cold means to you, the lesson is the same: When you step into harsh conditions unprepared, your entire system reacts.

Think about the last time you walked outside underdressed. A thin shirt, flimsy pants, a windbreaker doing the best it can. The cold slices through your clothes, stiffens your muscles, and demands your attention. You tense up. You move differently. Your thoughts narrow. You're not focused on the path ahead; you're focused on the discomfort around you. In that state, even a short walk can feel like an impossible journey.

But the problem isn't the weather.

It's the preparation.

On the days you dress for the conditions, like warm layers, a real coat, thick socks, insulated boots, the same temperature produces a completely different internal experience. The cold is still cold, but it doesn't destabilize you. You don't tense up. You don't shrink. You don't burn energy trying to simply withstand the moment. You move through the environment with what you've brought, not with what you wish you had.

Same weather.

Different experience, but this time, you were equipped.

That is exactly what the DO IT Change Method™ gives you.

DISCOVER is your weather report. It's the moment you stop pretending the conditions are something they're not and take an honest read of the emotional and situational climate you're facing.

OWN is the decision to take that forecast seriously. Instead of acting like you can muscle your way through the storm or pretend the cold won't affect you, you choose your posture, your preparation, and your mindset with intention.

IMPLEMENT is where you layer up. You don't suddenly become invincible, but you add what you need—a habit, a boundary, a mindset, a step—and those layers accumulate. Slowly, steadily, they build resilience. They prepare you for movement instead of survival.

TRANSFORM is the moment when you step into the very same conditions that once overwhelmed you and realize you're not overwhelmed anymore. The weather didn't change. Life didn't suddenly become easier or more predictable. What changed was you.

The DO IT Change Method™ doesn't eliminate storms or guarantee a smooth climate. It equips you. It gives you the emotional insulation and internal structure you need so that when life shifts, you're not standing outside in a windbreaker asking why everything feels so harsh.

Now you know how to adjust, respond, and stay steady enough to keep moving instead of bracing against every discomfort.

You don't need perfect conditions to move forward.

You just need to be prepared for the conditions you're in.

And now, you are.

You are stepping back into a world that will continue to change, continue to stretch you, and continue to present weather you didn't plan for. Now you meet it with a different internal climate, one that is warmer, clearer, steadier, and entirely capable of holding you through whatever comes next.

You are prepared.

You are equipped.

You are ready for your life.

You are ready to DO IT™

A Letter of Encouragement

Become Someone Your Past Self Could Never Have Imagined

Thank you for staying with this work. Thank you for choosing honesty over comfort, reflection over avoidance, and engagement over autopilot. Thank you for showing up to your life, chapter after chapter, even in moments when it would have been easier to look away.

I wrote this book because I believe something about you, and I want you to believe it too. You are capable of evolving into a version of yourself you haven't met yet—not a perfect or polished version, but a truer one. Someone who doesn't just survive change but participates in it, who doesn't just withstand discomfort but grows because of it, and who stops running from their future and begins walking toward it with intention.

A LETTER OF ENCOURAGEMENT

> I hope this stays with you long after you close this book: You are not meant to remain who you are today. We evolve.

Every month.

Every season.

Every stretch of life that asks us to become more honest, more grounded, more courageous than we've ever had to be.

And the version of you reading this right now?

You won't be the same in a year.

Or five months.

Or even five weeks.

The life you're moving toward is bigger than the limits you've carried, louder than the doubts you've rehearsed, and wiser than the mistakes that once made you question your worth.

I know what it feels like to question yourself. To replay missteps as if they define you. To wonder whether the version of you that faltered, froze, or fell apart is the version people will remember. Let me remind you that your mistakes are not your identity. They are not the final word on who you are becoming. They are moments that taught you, shaped you, and stretched you, but never limited you.

You are here because you have been willing to look at yourself honestly, choose differently, and rise again. If compassion exists for anyone navigating change, it exists for you, too. If grace is available to those learning how to become more of themselves, it belongs to you. And if there is hope for a life beyond what you've known, you are standing at the edge of it now.

So where do you go from here?

You keep evolving. You keep listening. You notice the small shifts and honor the quiet progress. You continue choosing the next aligned step, even when your voice shakes, and certainty feels just out of reach. And you remember that you do not have to navigate change alone.

While this book may be complete, your journey is not. The DO IT Change Method™ was never meant to be read once and set aside; it was designed as a rhythm you return to, a way of orienting yourself whenever life asks more of you than you expected.

> If I could leave you with one final thought, it is this: you are ready because you have grown, because you have learned how to return to yourself, and because you now have the internal skill set to move through uncertainty with intention instead of instinct.

Change is the invitation that carries you toward the life that has been waiting for you.

So go live your life—not just enduring what comes, but engaging with it. Participating in it. Shaping it. Growing through it. Becoming because of it.

I am rooting for you. I believe in you. I cannot wait to see who you become next.

Whenever you need a place to land, reflect, recalibrate, or rise again, DO IT™.

Resources & THE DO IT™ Ecosystem

Change doesn't end when you close a book.

You were never meant to navigate it alone. The DO IT Change Method™ is the foundation of an entire ecosystem designed to support you as you continue evolving. What you've practiced in these pages is the beginning. The tools, systems, and experiences below exist to help you deepen your understanding, integrate the work, and stay grounded through the seasons ahead.

1. The Change Archetype Assessment™

Discover Your Change Archetype

Just as every person has a unique personality, every person has a unique Change Archetype, the *patterns* that shape how you respond to uncertainty, decision-making, emotional activation, and internal transition. These patterns are not permanent traits or limitations; they are learned responses that can be understood, adjusted, and strengthened over time.

The Change Archetype Assessment™ identifies your Change Archetype so you can understand:

1. how you naturally react in transition

2. what strengths you bring into change

3. where your friction points tend to appear

4. how to best support your mindset, internal rhythm, and emotional system

5. what strategies will help you move forward with purpose

Your Change Archetype is a guide to making change easier, more intentional, and more aligned. **You can take the assessment at: www.mychangearchetype.com.**

2. The DO IT Change Method™ Workbook

Within these chapters, you've reflected deeply, told the truth honestly, and begun recalibrating from the inside out. The companion workbook gives you space to continue that work with:

- guided exercises

- reflection prompts

- implementation maps

- emotional regulation tools

- integration practices

- identity recalibration questions

It is designed to meet you in real time as life shifts, as your thinking evolves, and as your next chapter begins to unfold.

3. DO IT™ Live Workshops

If you want a deeper experience, the workshops offer immersive environments where you learn to apply the DO IT™ Method with real-time coaching, practical tools, and community support.

These experiences help you:

- regulate through discomfort

- shift old narratives

- build clarity around identity
- practice courageous action
- learn the emotional science behind your reactions
- expand your capacity for the life you're building

You don't have to transform alone. Growth happens faster and more sustainably when you have support.

4. Soleil Edge™ Programs

Soleil Edge™ offers a suite of programs for different stages and types of change:

The Soleil Shift — a six-week coaching experience for women who feel stuck and want to build momentum

Soleil Excel (Youth & Families) — emotional regulation, confidence, and resilience training for kids, teens, and parents

Soleil Exec (Leaders & Organizations) — leadership transformation, communication, executive presence, and strategic change support

Soleil Experience — retreats where grounded inner work meets lighthearted growth, designed to strengthen your identity, boost your confidence, and end with a tangible experience that lets your light take center stage

Each is rooted in the same philosophy that you **need the right support, and you are capable of more than you've ever been taught to believe.**

5. Continuing Your Journey

As this ecosystem grows, new tools will continue to emerge such as digital courses, advanced certifications, youth programs, corporate change labs, and future books designed to help you expand your capacity in every season. This work is more than a moment; it's a movement.

Stay connected with the DO IT™ community: www.doitchangemethod.com.

Reference Notes

Kübler-Ross Change Curve
Referenced in *Chapter 7* when explaining emotional fluctuations during change and the nonlinear process of internal adaptation.
Elisabeth Kübler-Ross & David Kessler, *On Grief and Grieving* (Simon & Schuster, 2005).

Fisher's Personal Transition Curve
Referenced in *Chapter 7* to illustrate the emotional oscillation between hope and doubt during personal transition.
John M. Fisher, *Managing Change: Personal Transition Curve* (2003).

The J-Curve in Organizational Transformation
Referenced in *Chapter 7* to explain the temporary performance dip before stabilization during major change.
Timothy J. Yeager, "The J-Curve Theory of Adjustment," *International Economic Review* (1999).

Bridges' Transition Model
Referenced in *Chapter 7* describing the "neutral zone"—the phase of ambiguity between an ending and a new beginning.
William Bridges, *Transitions: Making Sense of Life's Changes* (Da Capo Press, 2004).

Lewin's Unfreeze–Change–Refreeze Model
Referenced in *Chapter 7* to highlight the destabilization required before new behaviors take hold.
Kurt Lewin, "Frontiers in Group Dynamics," *Human Relations* (1947).

Neuroplasticity
Referenced in *Chapter 7* to explain how the brain forms new pathways when integrating new behaviors or emotional patterns.
Norman Doidge, *The Brain That Changes Itself* (Penguin, 2007).

Synaptic Pruning
Referenced in *Chapter 7* when describing how old neural pathways weaken as new ones strengthen.
Blakemore, S-J., "Imaging Brain Development: The Adolescent Brain," *NeuroImage* (2012).

Acknowledgements

There are seasons in life when you move quietly, doing the internal work no one sees. And there are seasons when the people around you become the scaffolding—steadying you, challenging you, holding space for you, and reminding you of who you are when the world feels uncertain. This book was written in the middle of both kinds of seasons, and it exists because of the people who stood with me through them.

To my husband, Kyle: Thank you for your strength, your patience, and your willingness to grow alongside me. This book was written during one of the most stretching seasons of our lives, and your steadiness gave me room to find my own. Thank you for creating a space where vulnerability is safe, where unraveling could lead to rebuilding, and rebuilding could happen without judgment. Your belief in me, especially when I struggled to believe in myself, lives between these pages. Your support didn't just hold me; it expanded me.

To my children: Your joy, curiosity, and honesty remind me what it means to evolve with grace. You've shown me that growth isn't linear, that love is sacred, and that change is meant to be embraced, not feared. Your innocence and resilience inspire me daily, and everything I build is rooted in the hope that you grow up in a world where emotional strength and self-trust are the norm. You are my reason, my grounding, and my reminder that becoming is a lifelong journey.

To my family: Thank you for your steady encouragement and unwavering belief. You are the foundation where my values were formed, my sense of belonging was built, and my confidence found its first place to grow. Everything I can create now began with what you poured into me then. Thank you for giving me roots strong enough to evolve and wings steady enough to rise.

To my mother: Thank you for pouring your whole heart into raising children who never doubted their ability to rise, because we knew you would be standing beside us. You gave everything to shape us into people with vision, courage, and confidence. The values you instilled continue to guide me through every season of my life and echo through every word of this book. I miss you, Mom.

To my father: Your ability to remain objective, even in the hardest seasons, grounded our family in ways I understand more deeply now. You taught me steadiness. You modeled how to stay centered when the world feels unpredictable. That stability shaped the foundation I stand on today. You always said we could stand on your shoulders, and I did. Thank you.

To my siblings: Your presence reminds me that growth is not meant to happen in isolation. We stretch, learn, and find our way forward as a unit, even as life carries us into different chapters. You are my first community, my original support system, and the people who know where I come from and accept who I'm becoming.

To the clients, students, and leaders I've had the privilege of working with: You are the true architects of this work. Your honesty, vulnerability, and courage to step into unfamiliar territory expanded the DO IT Change Method™ into something living and breathing. Thank you for trusting me with your stories and for allowing me to witness your evolution.

To every person who has ever felt stuck, overwhelmed, afraid, or uncertain: You are the reason this book exists. Your experiences, your questions, and your resilience gave language to this framework. Even if we never meet, I wrote this with you in mind to show you that with the right tools, you can shift, pivot, rise, and move into a chapter you once doubted was possible.

To my publisher: Thank you for believing in me from the moment we met. Not by chance, but by something that felt like fate. Thank you for championing this work and guiding it forward with both care and conviction. And to the editors, designers, and every person behind the scenes: thank you for lending your expertise, your precision, and your heart to shaping these ideas into something the world can hold, return to, and grow through.

Finally, to the version of me who started this book: Uncertain of where it would lead or what it would require, thank you for showing up. Thank you for continuing when it felt impossible and for uncovering depth you once overlooked. You became the first proof that this method works, and I am proud of you—more than you knew how to be proud of yourself at the time.

And to everyone who turns these pages and takes even one step toward a more honest, grounded, and empowered version of themselves: Thank you for being here. This book is yours now. May it meet you exactly where you are and carry you forward into who you're becoming.

Janine Lequay

Janine Lequay is a change strategist and the creator of the DO IT Change Method™, which offers a practical, human-centered framework built for navigating personal and professional transition with intention, stability, and agency. She specializes in helping individuals and organizations move through disruption without losing their internal footing or their sense of direction.

Before developing her signature method, Janine spent over a decade working in organizational change management, leadership development, talent strategy, and communication across complex corporate environments. With a Master's in Human Resource Management and as a certified executive coach, she has coached leaders, guided teams through restructuring, supported workforces during major transitions, and helped organizations understand the human side of change, including where resistance forms, how people adapt, and what supports lasting behavior shifts.

Her work sits at the intersection of **behavioral science, emotional intelligence, and practical strategy**, translating the patterns she witnessed in boardrooms, human resources departments, and lived human experiences into a framework people can use every day. She is known for her ability to make change navigable by helping people understand themselves within it.

Janine's perspective is informed by her own seasons of upheaval, rebuilding, and reinvention—chapters that demanded honesty, resilience, and a willingness to grow beyond what felt familiar. These experiences shape the compassion, strength, and practicality woven through her approach.

Through her writing, workshops, assessments, and the expanding DO IT Change™ ecosystem, Janine builds the comprehensive support system she believes every person deserves during transition, one grounded in tools, awareness, and skill sets we were never taught but have always needed.

She lives in South Florida with her husband, Kyle, and their three children, who remind her daily that growth is not linear, that identity evolves, and that change, when met with intention, can become one of the most powerful forces in a person's life.

www.ingramcontent.com/pod-product-compliance
Lightning Source LLC
Chambersburg PA
CBHW041039050426
42337CB00059B/5076